Anger Management for Adults

───── ❧❧❧❧ ─────

3 Manuscripts –
Anger Management,
Declutter, Mindfulness for
Beginners

Addison Fenn

Table of Contents

Anger Management **5**

*Control Anger & Stop Hurting the One
Person that Matters Most – You*

Introduction 9

Chapter 1: The Misunderstood Emotion 11

Chapter 2: Understanding Anger
Management 19

Chapter 3: Know Your Anger Style(s) 29

Chapter 4: Tools to Treat the Physical
Aspects of Anger 41

Chapter 5: Tools to Treat the Mental
Aspects of Anger 51

Chapter 6: Dealing with Anger in
the Long Term 63

Conclusion 71

Declutter **73**

Free Your Mind from Mental Clutter

Introduction 77

Chapter 1: Mental Clutter Defined 79

Chapter 2: Power of Perception 87

Chapter 3: Take Back Your Thoughts 93

Chapter 4: Mindfulness Meditation 99

Chapter 5: Three Principles
Psychotherapy 105

Chapter 6: Neuro-Linguistic
Programming 111

Chapter 7: Cognitive Behavioral
Therapy 117

Chapter 8: Minimalism 123

Conclusion 133

Mindfulness for Beginners 135

How Present Living Can Change Your Life

Introduction..139

Chapter 1: Why Mindfulness? 141

Chapter 2: Getting Started –
Mindfulness Meditation 147

Chapter 3: Mindfulness-Based Stress
Reduction..159

Chapter 4: Mindfulness-Based
Cognitive Therapy....................................165

Chapter 5: Commuting Mindfully 173

Chapter 6: Finding Mindfulness at Work.. 179

Chapter 7: Remaining Mindful at Home . 187

Conclusion.. 197

About the Author 199

Anger Management

Control Anger & Stop Hurting the One Person that Matters Most – You

Addison Fenn

Introduction

Congratulations on purchasing this book, *Anger Management: Control Anger & Stop Hurting the One Person that Matters Most - You*, and taking the first step towards dealing with an issue that has no doubt been plaguing you for quite some time. Admitting that you have an issue with anger is a difficult step to take, but unfortunately, there are far more steps ahead of you if you hope to squash your anger issues once and for all.

To help you along your way, this book will provide you with everything you need to start your journey towards a life that is no longer defined by anger. First, you will learn all about anger and how this much maligned emotion really gets a bad rap. Next, you will learn all about the basics of anger management and how you can start preparing yourself for a more productive future today.

From there, you will then learn about the major flavors of anger as well as basic ways to counter each. For even more useful techniques, you will find chapters devoted to both the physical and mental tools you can use to help yourself deal with anger in an effective way. Finally, you will find additional tips that will help you mange your anger in the long-term.

Before you get started it is important to keep in mind that everyone experiences anger differently, which means the techniques that work in countering that anger are going to be different as well. All this is to say that if one or more of the techniques suggested in the following pages don't work for you, it is important to not get discouraged and to instead put your head down and keep trying different suggestions until you find one that sticks. The right solution for you is bound to be here somewhere; as long as you don't get discouraged, you will have a new and improved relationship with anger before you know it.

Chapter 1:
The Misunderstood Emotion

Of all the emotions that a person can feel, anger is the one that can be the most difficult to pin down in the moment. There are times when you are angry that you feel as though you have never seen the world so clearly. As an emotion, you have no real control over when you feel anger but you do have control over how you respond to it, control that many people give up as an excuse to do something violent or dangerous and then not take responsibility for their actions after the fact.

Unfortunately, anger is often lumped in with violence and aggression, and those who have anger issues often make the mistake of writing it off without thinking about the many ways anger is a positive force as well. As such, the goal of this chapter is to shed some light on the most misunderstood emotion as the first step towards improving your relationship with it once and for all.

Anger has dimension

To many people, anger and aggression are one in the same, but this says more about the people who feel this way than it does about the emotion itself. Anger is actually far more varied than most people give it credit for. In fact, anger encompasses everything from the mild frustration a person might feel when they stub their toe all the way up to the all-consuming rage that they might feel when their pet is run over by a person on their smartphone.

While aggression often tags along with anger, it is its own distinct behavior that includes a very specific intention to do physical or verbal harm to a person or object. If you are currently dealing with anger issues of one type or another, it is important to understand the distinction as doing so is the first step towards taking back some of the power that you have no doubt given this emotion. Right now you may feel as though when you get angry the anger takes over, leaving you an unwilling participant in what comes next. This could not be further from the truth, however, and the rest of this book will show you how you can discover how to control the outcome of your actions or inactions.

Anger is predictable

Generally speaking, you can expect a person to become angry when faced with a situation that they see as either unfair or unpleasant. From there, they can be counted on to get even angrier if there is someone around whom they can blame for their predicament, or if it is clear the situation could have been prevented in the first place. If most people can be expected to react in the same way when presented with the same set of criteria, the question becomes why some people become so much angrier so much more often than others.

The answer is that everyone has a different threshold that indicates these criteria have been met. Those who have issues dealing with their anger have, for one reason or another, learned to take things to the extreme almost as soon as the option presents itself. For example, if someone cuts in front of you in line at the grocery store, you could either assume they did it on purpose, which is sure to cause anger, or you can assume they didn't see you and thus open the situation up to a host of additional possibilities.

Those who tend to lean towards the first assumption as opposed to the second may not even realize that there is a choice in the matter, which is why it can be so difficult for many people to come to terms with the fact that they have an anger problem in the first place. Once they come to an understanding that not everyone experiences anger in the same way they do, however, then additional progress can be made, but only if they are willing to work towards it. It is important to keep in mind that no change to something as major as the way anger is experienced can be completed overnight; this sort of thing can only come about with lots of hard work and dedication to success in the long-term.

There is nothing inherently wrong with anger

In the examples listed thus far, there is no reason to feel ashamed for feeling anger in the moment, as it is perfectly natural to feel angry when bad things happen to you that you didn't cause and that are out of your control. What's more, when anger helps people stand up to injustice or double down on their principals to create something better it can be a positive, productive emotion. No revolution was ever founded without anger and no innovation ever came about without someone first being angry at the status quo.

In fact, if you find yourself angry at something that you previously let pass without a second thought, then there is a good chance that your anger is a sign of personal growth, or at least that it can point out where personal growth is possible. If you find yourself growing angry at your current situation without understanding why, this can signify that it is time to take a closer look at the way your life is currently going to ensure that you are doing what you can to squeeze as much happiness from each day as possible.

Anger really is what you make of it, which means that it is up to each and every person to make the choice to express their anger in productive ways as opposed to giving in to the temptation to do something more destructive instead. When you feel a bout of anger coming on consider it a means of motivation, not a license to give in to basic instincts.

Unfortunately, for many people, the way they choose to express their anger often causes a variety of issues in their own lives and the lives of those around them. What's worse, the way they choose to express their anger actually ends up creating more anger in a vicious self-perpetuating cycle, as those who are the target of their anger begin to feel angry themselves.

When left unchecked anger is similar to cancer, in which it slowly infects every aspect of the angry person's life. It can cause them to lash out at their loved ones either verbally or phsyically, potentially leaving physical or mental scars that may never fully heal. While a brash young upstart might get away with getting angry at work at first, you can bet their career will stall when it becomes apparent that they can't contain their temper. Again, anger isn't responsible for all of these things but it is certainly the gateway to them, which is why it needs to be watched vigilantly to ensure that you always respond in a way that is beneficial for everyone involved.

Anger is more dangerous than you might think

While the worst case scenario for anger can be regularly seen on the news, there are far more insidious issues that it can take credit for as well. Known as maladaptive anger, this is the type of anger that leads to the destruction of one's personal property, substance abuse, or chronic verbal abuse.

It also leads to a wide variety of health issues, starting with undue strain on the heart. In fact, studies show that for two hours after you have a particularly angry episode your chance of having a heart attack doubles. This doesn't just mean incidents where you blow up and let your anger out in a verbal or physical way, as repressed anger can also contribute to heart disease. What this means is that while controlling your angry outbursts is a good place to start, in order to see true medical benefits from your new lifestyle you will ultimately need to learn to feel less angry in the first place.

In addition to putting extra strain on your heart, the two hours after a particularly angry outburst see an increased rate of stroke that is three times what it may normally be. For those who already have an aneurysm waiting in the wings, the risk of stroke increases to a whopping six times what it would otherwise be.

Beyond that, spending most of your time in an angry state actually weakens the immune system as your body is spending more time in a flight or fight state which requires additional energy, as opposed to in a relaxed state where it can prioritize general wellness. In fact, studies show that simply recalling a time when you were extremely angry can be enough to cause a dip in your antibody levels for upwards of six hours.

Chapter 2:
Understanding Anger Management

Now that you have a somewhat clearer idea of what anger is all about, you can surely see why you may have had difficultly dealing with the issue head on. In fact, due to its complicated nature, there is a whole industry built around handling anger management in the best way possible. This is not to say that the only way to get your anger under control is in a professional setting, however, as you may do just as well, if not even better, with a personalized anger management plan that you create yourself. Much like anger itself, the right plan is going to be different for everyone and the only way you can know if you are on the right track is if you give it a try.

Anger management programs

Anger management programs typically provide a very clear set of recovery guidelines for the person dealing with anger issues. More importantly, however, it also provides those who choose to go this route a controlled space where they can release their emotions without worrying about backsliding into less productive behaviors. It also teaches participants constructive outlets for their anger rather than the destructive ones with which they are too often already familiar.

Frequently, this process will include a detailed discussion of the unique things that trigger each person's anger, with a broader goal of teaching everyone to be more aware of their emotions at all times and at every level of anger severity. The goal is for them to ultimately learn to use these signs as a roadmap to help control their anger.

This sort of controlled therapy environment isn't just for those who are dealing with anger issues directly; it is also for those who are dealing with the fallout of having spent too much time with those whose anger issues remain unresolved. This is because anger revolves in circles: As one person takes their anger out on another, they too will likely become angry. And as such, this perpetuates more anger in the world.

The goal of anger management therapy is not to cure anger, but to simply provide those who are dealing with anger issues as many different options to dealing with their issues as possible. Anger management therapy tries to change how one responds to negative emotions. This is because reacting with aggression removes any legitimacy you have for being upset in the first place. It can also make it easier to look at situations from alternate, increasingly productive, angles.

Anger management therapy is available in both one-on-one and group settings, though the one-on-one sessions typically contain a group component as well. Individual sessions will likely address specific facets of the patient's anger issues including things like work-related anger, relationship issues, or issues with family. If you don't manage to get your issues under control successfully on your own, and you allow your anger issues to grow out of control, then you may find yourself in a situation where you are ordered to attend one of these types of classes by the court as the result of domestic violence or other legal issues.

Unlike some types of therapy, anger management classes have no firm amount of time or classes required. Rather, it will be up to the patient and the therapist to determine what issues need to be worked on and when the classes are ultimately no longer needed. It is common for many anger management classes to provide homework assignments or tasks for participants to complete while taking part in the program. These are designed to strengthen the techniques and principals discussed in the main class and ensure that the participant doesn't backslide throughout the week. More importantly, however, they allow the participant to practice what they have learned in real world scenarios.

The National Anger Management Association provides anger management courses across the continental United States as well as online. It is the leading agency when it comes to dealing with anger issues and it certifies everyone from psychiatrists to religious leaders to life coaches interested in effectively seeking out and dealing with these types of anger issues.

Unfortunately, while anger management therapy works for many people, it isn't a magic bullet that is going to cure these issues overnight, especially if they are based on learned behaviors that have been around since childhood. In order to benefit from these types of classes, you need to be willing to put in the work on your end and really want to change. Without a desire to improve you will only end up running in place.

Creating your own anger management plan

If your anger issues are not that serious, or if you simply prefer working through things on your own, then there is no reason that you cannot create a personalized anger management plan and work through it on your own. If you are going to go down this route, however, then it is important that you are ready to do some research and some soul searching to start. You will need to have a clear understanding of what your triggers are, the various levels your anger may reach and the signs of each, and tools that seem to help you step back from acting on your anger in an unproductive way.

Getting started:

Depending on how much time and energy you have already put into learning about your personal experiences with anger, you may be able to provide all the required information or you may not know where to start. If you are starting from square one, then you are going to want to keep a journal of your angry experiences so that you can learn from them and discover the patterns that you tend to follow time and again.

In your journal, you are going to want to include every instance where you feel angry, no matter how mild or brief the experience might be. You will then want to rate the intensity of the anger, note the situation that set it off, list the outcome of the feeling, how you responded and what tools (if any) you used to calm yourself down. It is important to be extremely honest with yourself when you are taking these notes as the only way you will be able to improve successfully is if you have a quality baseline to work from.

Once you have a month's worth of data to look at, you can start picking out obvious trends to your anger that should allow you to determine your anger type as discussed in the next chapter. From there, you will be able to determine the sorts of techniques and exercises that are more likely to work in defusing future situations. It is important to not limit yourself when it comes to trying different means of dealing with your anger as you never know when you might come across something that will literally change your life forever.

In addition to staying calm and in control at all times, you are going to need to ensure that you are still meeting your needs while at the same time not infringing on the needs of others. Once you have a handful of techniques that seem to work for you, and you have managed to defuse a number of potentially angry situations without losing your cool, then you will be ready to formalize your plan.

Analyzing your results:

Once you have the basic outline of a plan that appears to work for you in mind, the next step is going to be to analyze the results and see where you can improve. This means keeping detailed notes in your journal, even when you feel as though you are starting to get the hang of things. This will allow you to consider what is working and what isn't and, more importantly, where the techniques you have in your arsenal appear to be letting you down.

It is important to not let yourself get locked into anything without trying plenty of options, and also to not lose hope if things don't appear to be proceeding as quickly as you may have hoped. It is perfectly natural for you to come across techniques that seem to work in practice, only to have them fall apart in a real world scenario. Similarly, something you never expected to work based on practice can happen to do the trick when it matters most.

When everything is said and done, it is perfectly possible for you to have a wide variety of different plans that are tailor-made for specific events or scenarios. There is no reason not to be as experimental and creative as possible, after all, if you try something new and fail then you are no worse off than you were to begin with. Additionally, you might end up with an entirely new coping mechanism that you would have never thought of otherwise.

Always have a goal in mind:

Once you have the basics of your management plan down, all that is left for you to do is to come up with additional goals to ensure that you don't end up resting on your laurels and opening yourself up to the possibility of backsliding further down the line. While these goals can be anything related to your anger issues that you feel is worth tackling, it is important to put some thought into your choice for the best result.

In order to determine if a goal is worth your time, you are going to want to ensure that it is SMART. A SMART goal is one that is specific, which means you can clearly tell if you are on track towards success or failure. A SMART goal is measurable, which means it has any number of clear steps you can take to reach success. A SMART goal is attainable. While a goal of becoming the mellowest person on the planet is admirable, it is likely not going to happen any time soon so you should aim a little lower. A SMART goal is relevant; goals that will affect your life in a positive way sooner than later are always easier to stick with. A SMART goal has a timeframe, which means you want to set a date for your goal that is achievable, but not so attainable that it makes you lazy. Stick with goals like these and you will have your anger licked in no time flat.

Chapter 3:
Know Your Anger Style(s)

While it is true that everyone is going to experience anger differently, there are still going to be a wide variety of overlap, perhaps more overlap than you might think. Broadly speaking, anger can be categorized based on 5 different expressions:

- The objective of the anger (punitive or restorative)

- The level of impulsivity the anger causes (uncontrolled or controlled)

- The overall mode of the anger (verbal or physical)

- The reaction the anger causes (resistant or retaliatory)

- The anger's direction (external or internal)

Additionally, it is important to keep in mind that your anger might primarily manifest itself in different ways depending on the situation you find yourself in, whether that feeling is frustration, or a feeling of being disrespected and/or threatened. Don't forget, anger is neither good nor bad inherently; its negative reputation stems from the type of anger that some people use to express themselves. As such, clarifying the type of anger you are experiencing is a crucial first step when it comes to controlling the expression of your anger and thus your reactions.

Assertive anger

Of all the types of anger, assertive anger is the most productive. Anger of this type often expresses itself by taking feelings of rage or frustration and using them as a means for positive change. Instead of avoiding confrontation or resorting to physical or emotional outbursts, this type of anger often causes those who experience it to get to work to personally change whatever it is that caused the anger in the first place.

This type of anger is often an extremely powerful motivating force and it can be used to overcome a variety of other emotions, including extreme fear. The biggest challenge with this type of anger comes in harnessing it properly and taking full advantage of its motivating force, before the anger cools and you learn to live with the status quo.

Behavioral anger

This type of anger is expressed primarily via physical means, and those physical expressions can be extremely violent. Those who experience this type of anger often feel overwhelmed by their emotions, causing them to lash out at whatever it is that is causing them to feel angry. When left unchecked this type of anger can lead to violent confrontations and can often lead to negative and unpredictable interpersonal or legal consequences.

When it comes to controlling this type of anger, the best thing that can be done in the moment is to give yourself some space from whatever the focus of your anger might be. This will give you an opportunity to regain control mentally and use any number of the tools described in the later chapters to prevent yourself from doing something that you will very likely regret. While there are more permanent options you can certainly work on to ensure that your anger doesn't build to these violent levels, this simple and effective option can save you from countless mistakes you'd rather not make. Once you have calmed down, you will likely find that you can reconsider the situation from a completely different angle.

Chronic anger

If behavioral anger boils up in the moment, then chronic anger festers like a bleeding wound. Specifically, it refers to a type of generalized resentment of other people, circumstances, events or even the self that can last for weeks, months and even years. It typically expresses itself via habitual irritation, which can have serious negative effects on a person's health and wellbeing.

One effective means of starting to deal with this type of anger specifically is to take an honest look at what it is that is making you so angry – not just on the surface but at its root causes. While it may take some time, getting to the root of your resentment will mean that you are able to leave your anger behind once and for all. This often comes in the form of forgiveness for some past transgression which can bring about extreme emotional catharsis.

Judgmental anger

This type of anger often masquerades as righteous indignation, though it often goes farther than righting a true injustice and can be triggered by something minor like a perceived slight, or what is perceived as another person's shortcoming. While this type of anger makes it easy to assume you have the moral high ground in the moment, odds are you are being just as offensive to another person through how you treat their personal opinions. Judging someone that you don't know or someone who hasn't done anything against you is the most common expression of judgmental anger.

While this type of anger can be difficult to deal with in the moment, the best way to ensure that it eventually becomes less of a problem is by making a conscious, continued effort to put yourself in other people's shoes. What' s more, you need to make a habit of not just doing it now and then, but really committing to the practice every time you feel your judgmental anger on the rise. Depending on how set in your angry ways you are, this might be an extremely difficult exercise to get the hang of at first, but if you persevere it will get easier each time you manage to do so successfully.

Overwhelming anger

This type of anger is one that everyone experiences from time to time, as it occurs when you find yourself in a rough situation that is beyond your control. It often brings with it comingled feelings of frustration and hopelessness. While it is normal to feel this way when you suddenly realize that you have taken on too much responsibility and that there is no way to change course, or when unexpected life events beat you down, this type of anger can become disruptive if you start to feel it over more insignificant events. Once that happens it starts to make it difficult for you to function normally.

The feelings of hopelessness that typically come with this type of anger can make it extremely difficult to deal with all on your own. As such, if you feel as though you are feeling this type of anger to an unrealistic degree then it is important that you seek professional help.

Passive-aggressive anger

This type of anger is primarily used as an avoidance technique, letting the user vent their anger behind a guise of normalcy. Those who resort to this type of anger on a regular basis tend to try and avoid any and all types of conflict and may even repress or deny what they are really feeling, even to themselves.

Passive-aggressive anger often expresses itself through things like sarcasm, thinly veiled mockery and pointed silences but also via behaviors such as chronic procrastination. Depending on the severity of the denial, some people experiencing this type of anger don't even realize that they are actually being aggressive, making it difficult to self-diagnose and potentially leading to less than ideal professional and personal outcomes.

While it may take a third party to alert you to your passive-aggressive behaviors, once you are aware of the issue the best way to start to approach the issue is through learning more healthy and assertive means of expressing yourself. This should allow you to develop your ability to articulate things that make you angry or frustrated in a more confidant and productive fashion.

If you find that you resort to passive-aggression because you are afraid of the potential consequences, then the best way to deal with this issue is to follow your fear down the rabbit hole and see where it leads. If you are afraid of confrontation when standing up for yourself in conversation, for example, follow this train of thought to its logical conclusion and consider why exactly you are afraid. Whatever the issue is, odds are it has nothing to do with speaking your mind directly. Try to take the focus off the expression of the issue and put it on the root cause where it can be addressed.

Retaliatory anger

This type of anger can be difficult for some people to control because it often happens at an instinctual level in response to a direct confrontation or personal attack, whether verbal or physical. Everyone has felt this type of anger at one time or another as it is also the anger that flares up when you want to seek revenge over a perceived slight whether real or imagined. Retaliatory anger can be especially useful if you are justified in feeling angry in what you have suffered through as it can motivate you to right the wrong in a purposeful and deliberate fashion.

While it can be useful when it comes to helping you take control of a poor situation, it can also lead to thoughts of retaliation which can be especially disastrous if the inciting incident was imagined or the other party was unaware of the issue. Those who are under its negative influence may often try to intimidate others and force them to come around to their way of thinking rather than talking things through.

In order to mange the negative side of this type of anger effectively it is important to make a point of taking extra time to think before you act in scenarios where you feel yourself starting to get angry. If you are already aware of this issue then the few seconds of extra thought should be enough to short circuit the retaliatory nature of this type of anger long enough for you to consider if what you are doing is justified. Generally speaking, by making a decision to diffuse the current conflict you will find that you are able to avoid creating a scenario where revenge is the only option.

Self-abusive anger

This type of anger causes the person feeling it to lash out at themselves for perceived feelings of shame, humiliation, unworthiness or hopelessness. It is a type of anger that is fueled by shame and is typically expressed by self-destructive behaviors like eating disorders, substance abuse, self-harm or negative self-talk. Depending on their personal predilections, some people may instead lash out at those around them as a means of masking their feelings of low self-worth.

Due to the warped view of the world that often comes along with this type of anger, once truly internalized, it can be difficult to diagnose yourself with this type of anger. If you do come to the realization that you are holding onto to self-abusive anger then a great way to start working through your issues is via cognitive refraining techniques such as those discussed in a later chapter.

Verbal anger

While this type of anger is considered by many to be less dangerous than the more physical types of behavioral anger, the truth of the matter is that it can be just as harmful, if not even more so, than its physical counterpart. The issue here is that verbal anger leads to verbal abuse and the psychological and emotional damage that is done can potentially stay with the victims for the *rest of their lives*. Verbal abuse can be something obvious like loud shouting and threats of violence or it can be more subtle and be expressed as harsh criticism, unfairly placed blame, or ridicule. This type of anger is more commonly expressed in relationships and families.

The easiest way to deal with this type of anger is to work to get into the habit of gating the things you say based on whether or not you believe they will hurt the other person. While, at first, you may be tempted to blurt out the first hurtful thing that comes to mind, eventually you will find that you are able to realize what you say is going to have an effect on the person to whom you are saying it to and edit yourself accordingly. Once you learn to control the impulse to lash out when you are angry you can learn to express yourself through assertive anger expression instead.

Volatile anger

This type of anger seems to appear almost out of nowhere, manifesting itself in those who seem calm one moment and furious the next, regardless if they are raging about a life altering event or the waiter bringing them the wrong order at lunch. If you experience volatile anger then you may calm down quickly but the destructive potential of your anger likely means that everyone around you feels as though they need to walk on eggshells or risk your temper blowing up in unpredictable ways. If left unresolved, this type of anger can intensify to the point where you could seriously end up hurting yourself or others.

One of the most effective means of combating this type of anger is learning the signs that you are about to experience a volatile episode so that you can cut it off at the pass. Once you can properly identify what's about to happen, you can then take whatever mental or physical relaxation techniques that you respond to and put them to work.

Chapter 4:
Tools to Treat the Physical Aspects of Anger

Relaxation response

When stress floods the body in large quantities over a short period of time it triggers the body's flight or fight response. For those with anger issues either response may lead to feelings of anger. As such, if you fall into this category then you can likely short-circuit much of your anger by simply working on improving your relaxation response instead.

While you certainly won't be able to avoid every flight or fight response that gets in your way, by taking the time to learn how to enter a relaxation response at will, you should find that you are able to control your angry outbursts far more reliably than may otherwise be the case. The relaxation state essentially puts the brakes on the flight or fight response, and thus anything that happens as a result, and forces your mind back into a state of complete equilibrium.

This isn't just a mental response either: Having a true relaxation response will increase the flow of blood to the brain, relax your muscles, stabilize your blood pressure, normalize your heart rate, and slow your breathing. Beyond these measurable physical effects, this exercise will also temporarily boost productivity and motivation, enhance your problem solving abilities and even temporarily improve focus and increase energy.

There is no one right way to achieve a true relaxation response, which means everyone has their own perfect way to practice entering this state. The one caveat to this is that passive activities like reading a book or watching television, while certainly relaxing, aren't actually enough to generate the physical effects of a true relaxation response. The right relaxation technique is going to be one that focuses your mind and interrupts your regular stream of thoughts enough to elicit the type of physical response you should be aiming for.

Generally speaking, those who find they become angry in response to common stressors will often find more pleasure from things that are going to strive to calm them down. This can be things like guided imagery meditation, deep breathing exercise, progressive muscle relaxation or mindfulness meditation.

Deep breathing exercises

The key to getting the most out of deep breathing exercises is to start each breath from the abdomen to ensure that you are drawing in as much air to your lungs as possible. This is an important step as breathing from the abdomen as opposed to the upper chest will ensure you are getting more oxygen into your system with each breath, a surefire way to tell your body that you are not as stressed out as it might think. In short, the more oxygen you get in short order, the less anxious, angry and tense you will feel.

In order to maximize your breathing, the first thing you will want to do is to sit in a comfortable position with your back straight. Once you are in position, you will then want to place one hand on your chest and the other on your stomach. Next, breathe through your nose, ensuring that the hand on your stomach rises while the hand on your chest does to a much less degree.

From there, you will want to exhale through your mouth, making a concentrated effort to push out as much air as you can while at the same time actively contracting your abdominal muscles. Repeat as needed.

Progressive muscle relaxation

This relaxation exercise is actually a two-step process in which you make a concentrated effort to tense and then relax various muscle groups in your body. Doing so tricks your body into assuming that you are not currently in the midst of a flight or fight scenario because all of your muscles are so relaxed – and nothing bad ever happens when you are relaxed. As an added bonus, it will help you become extremely familiar with the feeling of tension that is likely to precede an angry outburst, particularly what it will feel like in specific parts of the body. This, in turn, will make it easier for you to remain vigilant against your triggers so that you can take the right precautions as needed. Finally, this exercise can also be combined with deep breathing for maximal results.

Before you begin practicing this exercise it is important that you first consult a doctor if you have a history of back problems, muscle spasms or other similar injuries that you feel might be inflamed by undertaking it. To start, you will want to find a comfortable position to sit in; you will want to ensure your clothing is relatively loose and that you aren't wearing any shoes.

When you are ready, you will want to take a few deep, calming breaths to clear your mind before focusing all of your attention on your right foot. Focus on the muscles in your foot and squeeze them as tightly as you can. Once you cannot squeeze any more you will want to hold that position for 10 seconds. Next, you will want to relax your foot completely for another 10 seconds, considering the difference between the two states as you do so.

You will then want to repeat the same process with your left foot and then continue in the same fashion until you have worked your way completely up the body. While initially you will likely have trouble only tensing the muscles that you are focusing on, with practice you should be able to successfully isolate the target areas. Ideally, each time you perform this exercise you will want to do an entire circuit of your body including your feet, calves, thighs, buttocks, stomach, chest, back, arms, hands, shoulders, neck and face.

Mindfulness meditation

Despite having been a part of various religious practices around the world for more than two thousand years, mindfulness meditation never really caught on in the western world until the 1970s when a number of studies started turning up measurable health benefits – not just to the mental wellbeing of its practitioners, but their physical wellbeing as well.

This, in turn, led to a renewed interest in the practice and a new understanding of the many ways that being mindful can improve one's health by directly getting to the heart of many of the issues that are caused by anxiety in the first place. With the backing of scientific studies, mindfulness meditation is now being used in a wide variety of governmental institutions in the United States including prisons and hospitals.

Practicing mindfulness will help you have a better understanding of your thoughts as something separate from your actions while also helping you to calm your mind, two things of vital importance when looking to improve the way you deal with your anger. While initially, you will want to practice being mindful in a controlled environment where you know nothing is going to interrupt you, eventually you will be able to practice it virtually anywhere and at any time. This makes mindfulness a useful choice when you need something to distract yourself from the current situation long enough for the anger to pass.

In order to get started, you will want to find a comfortable, quiet place where you can sit for between 10 and 15 minutes. To begin, you will want to take a number of deep, slow breaths. As you do so, you will want to consider how the air feels as it enters and exits your lungs, the sound it makes and the tastes it brings with it. From there, you will want to expand this awareness until it encompasses the rest of your senses as well. Your body is always providing you with a wealth of sensory information; all you need to do is make yourself available to it and you will be flooded with more sensory information than you might expect.

Eventually, your goal should be to get to a place where your mind is essentially blank. In the short-term, however, focusing on sensory information is a great way to block out the steady stream of thoughts that are, quite likely, always running through your mind. This is where mindfulness, when used in the moment, can help with anger issues as when used properly it can disconnect you from whatever it is that you are currently angry about for long enough to calm yourself down. For more information, consider my book _Mindfulness for Beginners: How Present Living Can Change Your Life_ where you can learn mindfulness techniques that you can use on the go.

Chapter 4: Tools to Treat the Physical Aspects of Anger

Medication

As with many psychological issues, treating your anger issues with medication is possible. While the goal should ultimately be to be able to function without this particular crutch, while you are working on learning more long-term management techniques there are many different over-the-counter (OTC) medications that can help you tone things down a notch or two.

Antidepressants including Zoloft, Celexa and Prozac are all regularly prescribed to help with anger issues. While they do not target the emotion of anger, they have a general calming effect that can help with several types of anger. As with any other type of medication-based treatment plan, it is vital that you speak with your primary care physician about your options and about what may well work best for you. After all, the purpose of medication is to complement the healing process, not complicate it.

In addition to prescription medications, there are a number of supplements and other over-the-counter medications that are known to help with anger issues to varying degrees. These include chamomile, passionflower and Valerian Root, as well as Proloftin and Benadryl. These last two are anti-allergy medications that are known to reduce anxiety as well. Both chamomile and passionflower can be consumed in tea as well as in tablet form to help stabilize mood and reduce anxiety. Finally, if you live in a part of the country where medical or recreational marijuana is a viable option then that is known to stabilize mood as well.

Chapter 5:
Tools to Treat the Mental Aspects of Anger

Emotional intelligence

Emotional intelligence (EQ) is the measure of a person's ability to properly identify and manage their own emotions as well as the emotions of others. As such, depending on the type of anger you experience, you may find that it is extremely helpful not only when it comes to controlling your anger but understanding it clouds your thoughts and provides you with alternative means of communicating whatever it is that is bothering you.

Broadly speaking, there are four main pillars of EQ that you are going to need to focus on if you hope to use it to reign in your anger once and for all.

Pillar 1 – Self-awareness

Self-awareness is, without a doubt, the most important of all of the aspects of EQ as without it you can never hope to understand your anger, much less pinpoint the triggers that are the most likely to set it off. Without being able to look inward and determine if what you find is the best version of yourself it will be difficult to ever improve.

Pillar 2 – Self-regulation

Self-regulation is a natural extension of self-awareness as once you are fully able to understand what it is you are really experiencing, it becomes far easier to reign in problem areas that you may not have previously given much thought. Essentially, improving your self-regulation is going to allow you to understand what makes you angry and helps you prepare for situations where you believe you are going to encounter your triggers.

Self-regulation is all about thinking before you act, which is another byproduct of self-awareness as once you are more aware of your baseline mental state then it becomes far easier to notice when things are out of whack. While it will be difficult to back off from your desire to express your anger in negative ways, with practice you will find that it is far easier for you to walk back from that edge. Finally, improving your self-regulation will also make it easier to put yourself in the other party's shoes, which has the potential to diffuse the situation right off the bat all on its own.

Pillar 3 – Motivation

Those with a high EQ tend to be motivated because they understand the many ways that thoughts influence actions. If you want to improve your response to anger but feel as though you don't really have the motivation to follow through the best way to go about getting started is by setting personal goals that are far enough away that you have to work for them, but not so far away that they seem impossible.

Pillar 4 – Empathy

Empathy is another important component of EQ as understanding what others are feeling better you will not only be less inclined to subject them to your anger, you will often find that you can come upon a solution that doesn't leave you feeling angry at all. Improving your empathy will also make it easier for you to refrain from judging others, and even yourself. There is no secret to improving your empathy; all it takes is making an active effort to see where the other person is coming from. While you may not always be able to see eye-to-eye, if you open yourself up to the opportunity then you are going to be able to find some common ground with almost anyone.

Triggers

Improving your EQ by working on the four pillars alone will also make it much easier for you to pinpoint the triggers that cause you to lose your rational mind to your anger. Everyone has triggers, things that happen either externally or internally that drives out rational thought in favor of acting with instinct. Luckily, improving your self-awareness and self-restraint will not only make it easier for you to spot your triggers but it will also make it easier to change what happens when your trigger "buttons" are pushed.

Take responsibility for your actions

When you are first working to improve your emotional intelligence you are likely going to find yourself getting angry more than you should be, and it can be easy to give up responsibility for what's happening and blame your actions on anger exclusively. Luckily, improving your EQ should help you to understand that while anger is an emotion that flares up in ways you may not always be able to control, the way you respond to that anger is very much something that you have control over. You need to strive to control your reactions to anger in order to prevent yourself from being a detriment to you and others.

It is important to keep in mind, however, that just because you start to successfully get your emotions under control does not mean that you are always going to have a firm lock on them. Emotions are finicky things and there is no reason that just because you have a lock on your anger in one manifestation doesn't mean it won't bust loose in another unexpected way. When you do lose your temper, it is important to not feel like a failure and instead understand that it is a natural part of the process.

Improve your reactions

Once you have become relatively proficient at understanding when your anger is starting to get the better of you, the next logical step will be to track the reactions you have to it as well. The simple truth of the matter is that many of the things that make you angry make most other people angry to one degree or another as well. The difference comes in the way that you respond to the anger, and once you start recognizing common reactions that you experience you can start taking proactive steps to change those reactions for the better.

Keep in mind, improving your EQ is not about hiding from your emotions; it is about processing those emotions as effectively as possible as soon as you realize what is about to happen. Never forget anger in and of itself is not a negative emotion, but it is how you have learned to deal with anger that is less than ideal.

Cognitive Behavioral Therapy

Cognitive Behavioral Therapy (CBT) is a type of psychotherapy that analyzes the response you feel to presented stimuli and then asks why it is that you feel the way you do. As your anger issues are caused by irrational responses to commonly seen scenarios, CBT is effective as it offers patients an alternative path back to healthy, realistic thought.

CBT operates on a few important principals, the first of which you should have no problem getting on board with: It is that the thoughts a person has will naturally influence both their actions and, over time, their behaviors as well. From there, it is all about changing thoughts to alter the actions that you take, both in the moment and eventually habitually as well. Therapists who practice CBT believe that everything is connected and nothing occurs in a vacuum.

The second important principal of CBT is that, from time to time, there are always going to be some things that happen that are legitimately beyond your control. Instead of obsessing over this immutable fact, CBT teaches that you should instead focus on the things that you can change as that is a far more productive use of everyone's time. This, in turn, will allow you to put your effort towards the things that will benefit you the most. Additionally, it is important to understand that actions, feelings and behaviors influence thoughts as much as thoughts influence behaviors, feelings and actions; which means that if you ever hope to truly be free of your anger you will need to break the cycle on all ends, not just when it comes to thinking peaceful thoughts.

Reinterpret the world around you

One of the primary things that keeps your brain busy all day is a constant struggle to make sense of all of the crazy things that are taking place around you at all times. CBT focuses on giving it new ways to interpret all of the data that you are constantly taking in at all times. No new thought ever occurs without passing through a filter of all your previous learned experiences. This means that if you ever want to break free of negative angry responses, you need to start from scratch by building a new response to common negative stimuli.

Unfortunately, this can be easier said than done. In order to deal with all of the information it is forced to process, the brain ensures that the actual processing power set aside to deal with thoughts is as streamlined as possible by running it through a filter of common thoughts, acts and experiences to determine if it is something you have seen or experienced before. If so, then the thought happens nearly automatically at an instinctual level. Currently, these thoughts are the reason that your default response is aggression or rage, but with lots of practice you can alter the way your brain thinks by default and insert new automatic thoughts in their place.

Keeping thoughts and emotions on track

As thoughts are almost always the cause of emotions, it is important to make an effort to not assume that everyone around you is always harboring some type of negative intention towards you. This one small change should go a long way towards keeping anger out of your default response list. After all, it is far more difficult to be truly angry at someone for an honest mistake then it is for a direct and personal slight. Then, with even more practice, you will find that you are able to replace the thoughts and actions that used to lead you to anger with more productive alternatives instead.

Assertiveness training

While you might feel as though those who are currently dealing with anger issues don't need any more help when it comes to asserting themselves, the fact of the matter is that assertiveness training can provide them with other means of asserting themselves that aren't so potentially harmful to everyone involved. After all, there is a difference between constantly being angry at everyone who stands in the way of your goal and using assertiveness to get what you want without alienating everyone else along the way.

This type of mental tool can be especially useful for those who deal with passive-aggressive anger as it gives them an alternative way to speak their minds without forcing them to step completely out of their comfort zones in order to do so. Perhaps unsurprisingly, true assertiveness has a lot in common with assertive anger in that it can be used to ensure that your rights are being respected and not being trampled by anyone else, either accidentally or on purpose. As such, if you find yourself easily hurt, betrayed, impatient, overly critical, or constantly annoyed with the world it may be a good idea to undergo assertiveness or personal boundary management training.

Chapter 6:
Dealing with Anger in
the Long Term

While your short-term goals should be all about managing any negative anger that you are currently dealing with, your long-term goals should be ensuring that when you do get angry it is a motivating force in your life, not something destructive. As such, once you have a personal anger management plan that works for you, your next goal should be letting go of any deep seated anger and just try to be happier in general. Happiness and anger are both emotions, and while it is possible to feel multiple emotions at once, which emotion do you want to ultimately lead your life?

Let it all go

If you are the type of person who has been dealing with anger issues for most of their life, then odds are you are holding onto old slights and grudges that can bring out your anger in an instant. As previously noted, old or imagined anger can be just as potent as anger over an event that is currently taking place which means that if you are ever going to truly live a life that is free of negative anger then you are going to need to make a conscious effort to let these memories go.

While this might seem easier said than done, this is because you have not yet made the decision to let the memories go, which lets them hang around compounding your anger over history with each new trip down memory lane. Do yourself a favor and think of the memory that causes you only a little anger, as it will be easier to start with. From there, work your way through the memory one last time, only instead of picturing it as vividly as possible, picture it as if it was recorded on an old VHS tape and the quality is extremely poor. As you watch, let the picture get fuzzier and fuzzier until it is indistinguishable from static. Then, picture taking the tape out of the VCR and placing it on a far shelf.

This visualization exercise can help you to put a cap on the memory and allow you to start building new mental pathways that don't involve returning to bad memories time and again. If you do find yourself thinking about it, simply picture yourself putting it back on the shelf and don't give it any additional thought. If you stay vigilant you will find that it is no longer nearly as relevant as it once was. You can then work your way up to more and more important memories as your familiarity with the technique grows.

Other more concrete techniques exist too for letting go of past events. I refer to these memories as "mental clutter", because all they do is fog your experiences and perceptions of reality. For more techniques, consider my book _Declutter: Free Your Mind from Mental Clutter_.

Verbalize your issues

For memories that are harder to shake, or for issues that you have caused because of your anger, you may find it especially cathartic to discuss the situation aloud with yourself or the person you wronged. You may want to write down your feelings or record them for an audio blog, whatever helps you really process what has happened. Understanding the true breadth of the situation using your greater knowledge of anger and how you can improve your responses should allow you to find closure in many cases.

While in some situations your anger may be largely justified, it is important to keep in mind that thinking in black and white only serves to increase the fuel that feeds anger in the first place. Even if another person wronged you initially, there are very few instances where one party is completely not at fault, especially if the event was serious enough that you are still holding onto it many years later.

Now it may be difficult to reopen old wounds in such an invasive manner, but it is vital that you power through if you ever want to get these issues off your chest once and for all. Never forget that your anger is only one part, an ever-decreasing part, of who you are. If you let it define you then you are giving it far more power than it deserves.

Don't be afraid to start small

After all the work you put in to getting to a point where you can focus on the long-term, know that small things that make you happy are equally important: Your general happiness can serve to keep anger at bay. It is no secret that anger gets in the way of love and happiness. Nevertheless, the simple truth is that making a concentrated effort to spend more time doing the things you love and taking care of yourself by eating right and getting enough sleep can make a huge difference when it comes to maintaining a generally positive attitude.

Exercise regularly

It's no secret that exercising releases serotonin into the brain which means you will feel happier overall. What's more, making exercise part of your regular routine will give you something new to focus on so that you don't suddenly feel at a loss as to what to do with yourself with your influx of free time – which you will have when you go from taking time to understand your anger and creating an anger management plan to actually implementing it.

The type of exercise that you pick up doesn't matter much: Committing to any sort of exercise will allow you to see results in a reasonable amount of time, which will encourage you to actually want to keep going with it. Not only will this ensure that your serotonin levels remain both high and stable, it will also keep giving you regular shots of positive reinforcement as all of your hard work starts to pay off in the form of real results.

What's more, this positive reinforcement should come with the positive results you are making day in and day out on your quest to conquer your anger. Tying something with more tangible results to the rather ephemeral nature of your quest to conquer your anger allows you to stack on your successes. As long as you keep up both conquests regularly you can think of your ever-improving body as the physical representation of all the hard work you are doing to improve your mental state.

Focus on the present

If you allowed your anger to get to a point where it enabled you to make serious mistakes then it can be easy to dwell on the past, regardless of what the present looks like. However, it is important to understand that if you stick with your anger management plan then you have come an extremely long way and no doubt took serious steps to distance yourself from the person you once were.

While it can be easy to dwell on the things in your life that you wish you could change, doing so will make it difficult for your mind to truly move on because you continue to invest yourself in the past. Instead, it is best to focus on all of the great things that you are currently doing to improve your life, and all of the things that you have to be grateful for. In fact, you should make a list every morning of the things you are most grateful for and carry it with you wherever you go. Then, if you feel yourself starting to return to your old ways, you can simply picture the things on your list and force yourself to think of everything that makes you happy instead. Over time, you will find the urge to be angry getting fainter and fainter.

In order to truly focus on the present or really consider the future, it is vital that you don't just lock your negative memories away; you need to also forgive *yourself* for the things that have happened in the past. While the degree of difficulty in this task will largely depend on the way your anger manifests itself, forgiveness is the only way you will be able to truly move forward. At the very least you need to be able to come to terms with the fact that if you had not done whatever it was that ultimately lead you to decide to take positive steps to improve your relationship with anger then you would not be the better person you are today. Don't forget, nothing happens in a vacuum: If a negative action ultimately leads to a greater positive response, then the negative action cannot be without some degree of merit.

Conclusion

Now that you have made it to the end of this book, *Anger Management: Control Anger & Stop Hurting the One Person that Matters Most - You*, you hopefully have a better understanding of the multifaceted nature of anger as well as your relationship with it.

While this book certainly includes plenty of tips to make your relationship with anger more positive, it is important to understand that anger is an emotion that will remain with you for the rest of your life. Far from a life sentence, it is important to remember the many things anger can do for you as well: If you are quick to anger over minor slights, then slights of injustice should be enough to get your blood boiling and help give you the drive to get out there and make a difference.

While it is certainly possible to get to a place where you can use your anger as a tool, it is important to understand that it is not something that is going to happen quickly. If you make the mistake of assuming that things are going to proceed at a rapid pace then you will only end up frustrated despite the fact that you are actually making a reasonable amount of progress. Instead of focusing on how far you have yet to go, focus on how far you've come and before you know it your rage will be a distant memory.

Declutter

Free Your Mind from Mental Clutter

Addison Fenn

express written consent from the Publisher. All additional rights reserved.

The information in the following pages is broadly considered to be a truthful and accurate account of facts, and as such any inattention, use or misuse of the information in question by the reader will render any resulting actions solely under their purview. There are no scenarios in which the publisher or the original author of this work can be in any fashion deemed liable for any hardship or damages that may befall them after undertaking information described herein.

Additionally, the information in the following pages is intended only for informational purposes and should thus be thought of as universal. As befitting its nature, it is presented without assurance regarding its prolonged validity or interim quality. Trademarks that are mentioned are done without written consent and can in no way be considered an endorsement from the trademark holder.

Introduction

Congratulations and thank you for purchasing this book – *Declutter: Free Your Mind from Mental Clutter*. Mental clutter is an insidious threat to your mental wellbeing that is made all the more dangerous by the fact that it could be lurking in your mind right now – clouding your mind, manipulating your thoughts, and zapping your motivation without your knowledge.

Luckily, the following chapters will discuss everything you need to know in order to combat this virulent menace. First, you will learn all about mental clutter, how to spot it, and why it is important to cut it out of your mind whenever you find it. Next, you will learn about increasing your natural abilities of perception as well as the need for doing so when it comes to remaining vigilant against mental clutter. You will then learn some basic tips for taking back your thoughts, including how to combat negative self-talk with a more positive alternative. You will also learn about the many benefits of mindfulness meditation, both in general and as it relates to mental clutter.

From there, you will learn about a variety of different types of therapy and how they can be used to deal with particularly stubborn bits of mental clutter. First, you will learn all about the Three Principles, and its unique type of related psychotherapy that teaches the fact that nothing about a given traumatic event actually matters. You will then learn about neuro-linguistic programming and the ways it believes everyone's experiences are subjective. Next, you will learn about cognitive behavioral therapy and the ways it can help you deal with leftover mental clutter once and for all. Finally, you will learn all about the benefits of minimalism and how clearing out physical clutter can help clear out the mental clutter as well.

As a disclaimer, this book is not about physical clutter. If that is what you are looking for, I suggest taking a peek at my book – _Declutter: Organize Your Home and Free Your Life from Physical Clutter_.

Chapter 1:
Mental Clutter Defined

Generally speaking, the word clutter conjures up images of piles of unidentified "stuff" sitting hither and yon waiting to be dealt with in one way or another. While it can be annoying at times, it is generally thought to be largely harmless – assuming you watch your step that is. While easy to avoid in small amounts, the nature of clutter is that, if left unattended, it will only multiply over time until you eventually find yourself staring at the type of mess you can only deal with by devoting an entire weekend to the task. Hence why most clean and minimalist homes obey the clear surfaces rule: Clutter multiplies, and they multiply quickly.

In much the same way as a pair of old shoes here and an Amazon shipping box there can eventually turn a closet into a wasteland, mental detritus – such as bad habits, incorrect attitudes, emotional baggage, unresolved grudges and the like –can lead to mental clutter. If left unresolved, mental clutter can lead to the types of negative personal patterns that make things like undue struggle, extreme stress, suffering, and personal-sabotage more common occurrences. Simply put, mental clutter can be thought of as the stuff that sets you at odds with the world around you.

Looking for symptoms of mental clutter

One of the most nefarious parts of mental clutter is the fact that many of its aspects serve to mask the fact that there is an issue in the first place. As such, if you have let your mental clutter build up unchecked for years, then you may be extremely cluttered without even realizing it. If you are worried that this is the case, consider the following list of symptoms and see if they apply to you.

- *Increased confusion:* Do you find yourself frequently confused by things that you used to handle with ease? Senses of general confusion, often accompanied by either fear, worry, or both, as well as a general sense of feeling scatterbrained are signs that you may be dealing with an influx of mental clutter.

- ***Chattier inner voice****:* Everyone has a mental narrator who operates in the back of their mind to some degree. If that voice seems to never shut up, then you may be dealing with an influx of mental clutter. If your inner dialogue goes from normal amounts to what amounts to a constant noise in the background, then this should be considered a red flag that you potentially have mental clutter.

- ***Increased chaos****:* While there are always going to be certain events in our lives that sow disorganization and chaos when they appear, this should be the exception and not the rule. As such, if you find that you are always dealing with a large amount of chaos in your life, either physical or mental, then you may need to take a closer look at your mental clutter and see if that isn't part – or all – of the problem.

- ***Increased conditions or rules****:* When it comes to mental clutter, having an influx of conditions can also be thought of as having lots of requirements, stipulations, or prerequisites on your daily routine or the activities and events you take part in most frequently. If lately, you have been feeling as though everywhere you turn there are limits, rules, and boundaries, either external or internal, then you may be dealing with an influx of mental clutter.

- ***Increasing desire to collection things***: If you are someone who has always had had collections, then determining if your desire to collect have gotten stronger can be difficult. The issue here is that a build up of mental clutter can lead to a desire to stockpile trophies or other physical representations of validation you have received in hopes of feeling additional comfort or security. This is a prime example of how your mental state can affect the physical world: A cluttered mind creates a cluttered environment. As such, it can be helpful to consider if you have recently started a new collection or have started a new round of expansion on an existing collection.

- ***Comparing yourself to others***: If you tend to be happy, generally speaking, with your lot in life only to recently find yourself comparing what you have to everyone else, this could be a sign that your mental clutter is on the rise. This typically occurs as an offshoot of the desire to seek out bigger and better things on the horizon and often indicates an underlying issue elsewhere instead.

The worst of the worst

While every type of mental clutter has the potential to be dangerous, there are three types that can be particularly damaging. They are worry, guilt, and negative self-talk.

- *Worry:* Worry is potentially the most harmful type of mental clutter as it can not only make the leadup to a given experience miserable, it can actually limit your full potential and make the negative outcome you were so afraid of actually come to pass. Worry also makes it easy to fall into the trap of only thinking in absolutes, when in reality things are far more varied. This also leads to more rigid thinking, which can make it more difficult to utilize either creativity or problem solving.

- *Guilt:* Guilt is a tricky bit of mental clutter: If you give into guilt once, it can be easy to become trapped in a prison where your worst mistakes are played on a loop while you are forced to wonder about what you could have done differently. When handled unproductively, this leads to an endless cycle where the only outcome is despair, giving off the illusion that it seems as though there is no point in trying anything new.

- *Negative self-talk:* The beliefs you have about yourself and the world around you can profoundly alter the way you see the world. As such, negative self-talk is a symptom of mental clutter that has the potential to color everything you do if you aren't careful.

If left untreated, mental clutter has the potential to throw you out of harmony with your thoughts. It can also lead to a lack of harmony in the world at large, as well. It can start off as a feeling of mental fog and can easily evolve into a form of malaise that can last for weeks, months, or even years. Along the way it cripples the potential of the victim in all facets of their lives, filling them with doubt and mistrust about those around them and their own abilities to make it in the world at large. This is why it is so important to be on the lookout for mental clutter and to be prepared to nip it in the bud whenever it is found.

Chapter 2:
Power of Perception

As previously noted, spotting mental clutter can be difficult, especially at first. As such, one of the first things you are going to want to do in order to fight it successfully is going to be improving your powers of perception. The things you choose to notice, or choose to not notice, go a long way towards framing how you see the world as a whole. As such, if you have developed bad habits over the years when it comes to perception, it is best to work hard now to rewire your brain and really notice the world. Perception is reality, after all. And you never know what you might find that was literally hiding in plain sight the entire time.

Pay closer attention

With the proliferation of screens across all forms of technology, people are increasingly being rewarded for dividing their time among as many different tasks as possible. As a result, there is far less time to focus on the smaller details of a given situation and consider the types of meaning that are only found upon closer consideration. Therefore, the first step in becoming more perceptive is going to be taking note not of what you are missing, but of the fact that you are missing something.

To get started down this path, all you need to do is stop for a few moments once or twice a day to consider what is really going on around you and to think about how much you are currently missing out on throughout the day. The specifics here don't matter, as long as you slow down and take the time to look at life from another angle. This could include something adventurous like hiking a new trail every weekend, or it could be something simple like making a point of noticing what your coworkers are wearing each day. Alternatively, you can point your perception inwards and try to figure out why you feel the way you feel at certain situations. Again, the specifics don't matter as long as you work on it each day and start building this new skill in the process.

Take notes

If you find that, despite your best efforts, you don't seem to be making much progress, you may find that taking field notes as if you were a scientist in the wild helps you focus on the problem at hand. If you get into the habit of taking notes about whatever it is that you are doing, you will find that you naturally start paying attention to smaller details you may have otherwise missed as a result. The best part is you can practice this exercise virtually anywhere, at any time. Observe your coworkers for a few minutes during your lunch break, and observe your children when they get home from school. Any time you are observing the behaviors of others, you are gaining tools that can help you to be more perceptive about yourself as well. The opposite is true too: If you are being observant of your own behaviors, you can use that to be more perceptive about other people.

Throw in critical thinking

After you get into the habit of more closely observing the world around you, the next step is to start using these observations to come up with well-reasoned ideas or working theories.

Declutter

Successful deduction based on your observations is all about thinking about a given situation logically and then applying those observations to what you are seeing. One part is about observing closely, and the other is about acting on those facts.

Once you have gotten into the habit of observing things more closely, building up your habit of deduction is as easy as thinking critically about anything new that you learn. Putting a little extra thought into every fact you learn will ultimately make it easier to put yourself under the microscope and analyze your behavior when it comes to looking for signals that indicate mental clutter has taken over your mind.

Extrapolate

Once you have gotten into the habit of both being more observant and putting together deductions based on what you have seen, the final step is to bring it all together and use what you have deduced to make other, longer reaching assumptions about whatever it is that you have been observing. This is what is known as maximizing your mental real estate. Essentially, the more connections you make between otherwise disparate points of information the more tools you will have when it comes to thinking critically and the more effective the deductions you make will be.

When it comes to putting the full spectrum of perception to use on yourself, once you are comfortable with extrapolation you will be able to use it on yourself to pinpoint issues you may be having and understand how they are related to the larger issues you may be dealing with. This, in turn, will make it far easier for you to stop fighting with the symptoms of your issues and start dealing with the issues themselves directly. Simply put, the sooner you increase your natural perceptiveness, the sooner you can get started decluttering your mind once and for all.

Chapter 3:
Take Back Your Thoughts

Once you have managed to successfully what is clouding your thoughts, the next step is to work on clearing out your mental clutter by clearing your mind. Try the following to do just that.

Understand the power of distraction

Scientists out of Brown University have recently released findings from a study that shows that one of the best ways to remove unwanted thoughts from your mind is to occupy your thoughts with something else instead. The study found that the various regions of the mind could align in thought when thinking about either the right hand or the left hand but had far more difficulty thinking of both at the same time.

You can put this fact to work when it comes to taking back your thoughts from mental clutter as soon as you have identified the types of mental clutter you are dealing with. Once this is done, you will then be able to focus on what your mental clutter is trying to force you to ignore. Focusing on the underlying problem of the matter – instead of the symptoms – will make it more difficult for anything else to get through, allowing you to gate your thoughts as a result.

Utilize substitution

If you can't distract yourself from your mental clutter using cold hard facts, you may instead find success by using your imagination instead. Specifically, you may be able to convince yourself that things aren't really as bad as they seem to be by putting on your rose-colored glasses. While this might seem like a less than ideal solution, studies from Cambridge show that if you believe hard enough pretending actually activates the same region of the brain as when you know something is true. In fact, this is how lie detectors work: Lie detector tests can only detect whether someone truly believes in what they say – not whether what they say is true or not.

With this in mind, it then becomes far easier to deal with your mental clutter once you have identified it. For example, if you constantly find yourself stacking up poorly against your peers, you simply have to believe that you are good enough and your previous beliefs and comparisons will fade away. While you may not see results overnight, you may be surprised at how effective this practice can actually be as it slowly rewrites your neural pathways.

Increase physical activity

This technique is simple. If you make the time to get out and get your blood pumping, you will find it far easier to focus on the task at hand. As such, if you find yourself feeling overwhelmed by your mental clutter, you can find an easy break from the chaos by taking the time out to exercise. By physically separating yourself from the issues at hand, you will find that it is easier to mentally let go of the issue as well. As an added bonus, you will find that the extra boost of endorphins that are released at the same time will also serve to improve your mood and decrease your levels of stress.

Spend more time being grateful

When you find yourself feeling overwhelmed by all of the mental clutter that is clogging your mind, taking a few minutes to focus on all the things in your life you are grateful for can help you put everything in perspective. You may want to consider certain aspects of your life you are grateful for in the moment, or you could even simply list off the things you are thankful for. The act of simply taking stock of your needs should be enough to clear your mind, at least in the short-term, and can help you get things back on track afterwards.

Dealing with negative self-talk

When working through your mental clutter, one thing you will eventually need to deal with is any negative self-talk that you have been abetting despite your best interests. Everyone has a little voice inside that whispers that they may not be fast enough, strong enough, smart enough, etc., to complete a given task. Most people are able to keep that voice relatively quiet, but those who are dealing with lots of mental clutter have no such luck. As such, their negative self-talk runs wild, making it more difficult to clear out their mental clutter overall.

Luckily, negative self-talk can be directly countered with positive self-talk. Positive self-talk is an exercise that helps clear out the types of mental clutter that supports negative self-talk, and it can be used whenever you find yourself being particularly down on a thought or action you are attempting. To get started, all you need to do is to be aware of a negative thought that is taking place and strive to replace it with a positive thought instead. It is important that you strive to deny the thought before you replace it for the best results.

While this may not feel particularly productive at first, it is important to keep it up if you hope to see serious results. Eventually, you will find that you are able to break yourself out of negative self-talk by simply being aware of what it is your mind is trying to do. Even better, with enough practice, you will be able to replace negative self-talk with positive self-talk which will ultimately go a long way towards altering your mindset for the better.

If you find that you have a hard time with this exercise at first, don't despair; many people grew up in environments that make it difficult to express themselves without feeling awkward, you just need to persevere. If you find that you have a hard time substituting in positive thoughts for negative ones, try writing these substitutions down in a journal first to help you get the hang of it. When writing, all you need to do is look for phrases containing words like "can't" or "won't", and then you simply replace them with positive alternatives instead. With practice, this will clear your mind of all sorts of mental clutter.

Chapter 4:
Mindfulness Meditation

While it comes with a wide variety of additional mental and physical benefits, at its core mindfulness meditation is all about striving to become as connected to the moment as possible in hopes of bringing additional clarity and focus to your mind as a result. Mindfulness meditation is extremely simple to learn, though difficult to master, and can be done virtually anywhere and at any time. What's more, it can be used to help you remove all types of existing mental clutter, while also helping prevent new clutter from forming in the future.

To give it a try, all you need to do is focus on taking long, deep breaths and trying to take in as much of the information that your senses are providing you with as possible. While it sounds simple when written out, odds are you found it more difficult to clear your mind of outside thoughts than you anticipated. Nevertheless, making a habit out of practicing it for as little as 15 minutes a day can not only help you with your mental clutter, but also aid you when it comes to improving your overall sense of self. Mindfulness meditation will also reduce your overall levels of stress.

When it comes to practicing mindfulness meditation successfully, it is crucial that you avoid making the mistake of giving every stray thought that comes to your mind the power to derail the meditative process. To prevent this from happening, you may find it helpful to visualize all of your thoughts passing through you, each encased in its own bubble. Instead of interacting with each new thought that floats into your mind, simply watch it float by without doing more than acknowledging its existence. You may also find it useful to visualize your thoughts as the flow of water out of a faucet that you have the power to turn off.

The following is a step-by-step guide to mindfulness meditation.

Step 1: Make time

A famous mindfulness saying states that if you have the time, you should practice being mindful for 15 minutes a day; however, if you don't have time, then you should practice for 30 minutes per day. This is to say that the more hectic your life is the more benefit you can find in mindfulness mediation and why it is so crucial that you fit it into your schedule and never waver. This will become easier after you get the hang of things as you can practice being mindful virtually anywhere.

For starters, however, it is best to set aside some time each day to find a quiet place where you won't be bothered for at least 15 minutes. As with any new habit, it is important to stick with it regularly for at least 30 days if you really want to make it a part of your routine. Since it is a low-impact practice and nothing external is required, this makes it easy to fit into a busy schedule but it also makes it easy to put off until later too. You will need to consider the potential benefits and make a commitment to being mindful if you hope to clear your mental clutter once and for all using meditation.

Step 2: Become one with the moment

While quieting your mind of stray thoughts is certainly helpful the real goal of mindfulness meditation is to focus completely on the moment, without forming judgments about any of the things you find. When you judge an experience, it becomes far easier to dwell on it, which will take you out of the moment as a result. While avoiding judgment is easier said than done, it is a crucial step when it comes to mastering mindfulness and it definitely becomes easier with practice. When you do find yourself passing judgment don't dwell on the fact and compound the problem, but simply let the thought go and return to the moment.

Step 3: Always return to the moment

Mindfulness meditation is the art of bringing yourself back to the moment, over and over again, as many times as it takes. It is extremely easy to get lost in a given thought and pull yourself out of the moment as a result, which is why it is important to never get discouraged. Especially early on, it is perfectly normal for your mind to wander after only a few minutes of being mindful. When this happens, all you need to do is double down and, with time, you will find that the entire process becomes far easier.

Other opportunities to be mindful

Being mindful doesn't have to be limited to only when you meditate. There are many opportunities to be mindful outside of meditation. Here are some examples.

- *Showering*: While many people operate on autopilot while in the shower, you can use this opportunity to give yourself a boost of mindfulness instead. This is because the senses are already in overdrive in the shower, which means it is easier to get into the moment than it may be in other situations.

- *Exercise*: While it might seem surprising, the mental state that the body finds itself in while exercising – specifically cardiovascular exercise – is actually quite close to a state of mindfulness, which means it doesn't take much to push it over the edge. To get in the zone, consider the way your body feels as each muscle exerts itself as you push it to the limit.

- *Chores*: The repetitive nature of most chores makes them a perfect outlet for a bit of mindfulness. To make the most of these tasks, all you need to do is clear your mind beforehand and then focus on all the sensations working through the task provides you. When you are finished, consider how much better off you are now that the chore is completed and reflect on your ability to positively affect your environment.

- **_Social media_**_:_ Making a more concentrated attempt to single-task will ultimately help you practice mindfulness more easily. Until you decide to do away with social media distractions completely, consider using them in a more mindful manner instead. The next time you find yourself looking through your old photographs, use that time to really remember the moment that each photograph was taken. Strain your memory and try to recall everything you can about the situation. What were the smells, the sounds, the sights? How did you feel in the moment? Really work to try and get back to that place, to the extent that you block out external stimuli.

Chapter 5:
Three Principles Psychotherapy

The ideas behind the Three Principles of Mind, Consciousness, and Thought were first spoken about in the 1970s by a man named Sydney Banks. Also known as the concept of Health Realization, proponents believe that the Three Principles fully explain human experience as the sum total of emotion and behavior.

The Three Principles and how they relate to removing mental clutter are described below.

- *Mind:* Mind can also be thought of as the intelligence and energy of life in all its forms. This energy comes together to form what is known as the Universal Mind, which is constant and immutable. This represents an ideal state where the mind is at peace and free from any dissenting outside influences. It is directly contrasted by the state of perpetual change that is promoted by excessive mental clutter. The goal, then, is to improve over time and move from one state to the other.

- **Consciousness***:* Consciousness can also be thought of as a form of heightened awareness. Within the Three Principles it allows for the recognition of form, which is the physical expression of thought. However, when it comes to dealing with mental clutter, you would want to increase your consciousness for the same reason you were encouraged to increase your perceptiveness in Chapter 2. Specifically, being more aware of your thoughts will make it easier to determine when mental clutter is building so that you can take proactive steps to stop it in its tracks.

- **Thought***:* The Three Principles teaches that the power that lies within all thought is not created internally; rather, all thought is a divine gift which is given to each person when they are born. Thought is the creative agent that is used to give meaning and direction to life, and this is true when it comes to clearing out mental clutter as well. Only with a purity of thought and clarity of purpose can you hope to banish mental clutter once and for all.

Three Principles Psychotherapy Explained

If you are having difficulty clearing your mental clutter on your own, then you may want to consider psychotherapy based around the Three Principles as a means of jumpstarting the process. The biggest difference between traditional psychotherapy and Three Principles psychotherapy is that, with traditional therapies the problems and feelings that people have are addressed individually as relevant issues that can be solved in a variety of ways.

While that all sounds pretty straightforward, when it comes to Three Principles therapy the problems and feelings and individual experiences are instead essentially thought to be an illusion created by Thought and forced into reality by Consciousness. As such, Three Principles psychotherapy posits that the solution is to see these problems and feelings for the illusions they are through new insight gained from personal reflection.

To understand the differences found in a Three Principles therapy session, it may be helpful to look at the difference of approach when one uses cognitive behavioral therapy, which is discussed in greater detail in Chapter 7.

For starters, the therapists practicing cognitive behavioral therapy would seek out the primary event that likely led to the symptoms that are being presented, treating each as a different fact that the client would need to deal with in order to resolve the issue successfully. This event would then become the focus of the treatment, at least for a time, and the way the client responds to the event would indicate how therapy would proceed.

On the other hand, a Three Principles based approach would instead view the incident in question as having no special importance to the way therapy progresses as a whole. Likewise, negative reactions to the event would not be seen as having particular relevance to the event, but rather indicating the client's current understanding as to how Thought played a part in determining their outcome in the experience.

From there, treatment becomes about the therapist helping the client find personal insights regarding the way their thoughts played into the perception of the incident in question. Ideally, they will learn that the only true reality is the one that they experience, as well as what they enable others to experience at the same time. What's more, they will hopefully learn that this perception of reality isn't fixed in any given moment and instead is as fluid as they can make it.

These types of insight prove far more manageable when the client feels relaxed and comfortable with the therapist, as well as with the therapy itself. This will allow them to start on the path to clearing their mental clutter, as effectively as possible. Finally, treatment will turn towards giving the client the ability to transcend any individual event, to find the creative power of thought and utilize it to build a mind that is only focused on achieving the goals set out for it.

Chapter 6:
Neuro-Linguistic Programming

Neuro-linguistic programming, or NLP for short, is a type of psychotherapy that was created by a pair of researchers in the 1970s by the names of John Grinder and Richard Bandler. They claimed to have found a connection between neurological processes in the brain, behavioral patterns, and language that needed to be tweaked sufficiently in order to find ultimate success in life. NLP also functions under the assumption that one person can model the skills of a highly skilled person to acquire those skills for themselves.

It is easy to see how NLP can benefit those who are having difficulty clearing their minds of mental clutter for multiple reasons. First, the neurological processes that it takes into consideration are often related to various types of mental clutter and, as such, addressing them directly brings them into the open where they can be more easily removed. Second, the modeling theory allows those who seem to constantly be building up new mental clutter to model their behaviors on those who can manage to keep a clean mental shop and improve their own mental space as a result.

Core concepts

The basics of NLP can be distilled down into three key concepts: subjectivity, behavior, and consciousness.

- *Subjectivity*: According to NLP everyone experiences the world subjectively, which means that everyone's experience is going to naturally be subjective as a result. These subjective experiences are then broken down in terms of the five senses, as well as the language that is available to accurately describe them. As such, if you remember an event, you remember the experiences you had before chaining them together with language to make them into a story you can remember. Mental clutter can affect this recollection which is why NLP can be useful in dealing with the issue in a more permanent fashion.

- *Behavior:* The idea behind behavior can best be understood in terms of the sense-based subjective representations that occur as part of each person's subjective experiences. NLP then posits that personal behavior can then be modified through a manipulation of the subjective experience to successfully clear the mind of mental clutter.

- *Consciousness*: NLP believes that consciousness is split into conscious and subconscious components. All subjective experiences are naturally subconscious experiences and the goal is to make them more conscious, allowing you to take control of the experiences. This will also remedy any issues behind your mental clutter in the process.

Other important aspects of NLP are modeling, submodalities, and representational systems.

- *Modeling*: Modeling is the process of adopting the strategies, language, behaviors, and ultimately the beliefs of another, exemplary, person in order to model what they do in hopes of obtaining a semblance of their success. NLP modeling methods are designed to make it possible for the practitioner to subconsciously assimilate the knowledge the exemplary person has to improve their own experience. Once the practitioner is capable of modeling their subject's patterns, it then becomes easier to alter existing belief patterns so that they align more naturally with the new thoughts and habits. This can be effectively used to deal with issues that are leading to mental clutter that you just can't shake off through more traditional means.

- **Submodalities**: The relative strength of a given experience can be broken down into specific submodalities that involve measuring the level of brightness, size, volume and the like, of internalized sensations. A typical method of changing a submodality involves manipulating the way it is expressed in the memory, removing any mental clutter that was originally associated with it in the process.

- **Representational systems**: The idea that experiences are processed and codified via sensory systems was first posited in gestalt therapy and added to

NLP shortly after its creation. It teaches that memories are closely linked to the sensory experience of a given event, which means all of the information about that event is stored in those sensory experiences. Anytime you recollect a memory, the memory is represented through the sensory experiences you stored – which can alter your current mood when the memory is resurfaced. This is why thinking about sad thoughts can make you feel sad. Some representations are going to be processed consciously, but most are processed subconsciously.

As such, by matching the desired outcome with a preferred style of representational system, a practitioner could affect their perception of a given experience for the better. When done properly, it can help clear mental clutter and ensure that it doesn't creep back in at a later date.

Chapter 7:
Cognitive Behavioral Therapy

Cognitive Behavioral Therapy, CBT for short, works based on the assumption that not all thoughts and behaviors can be controlled by conscious thought and will alone. Instead, it posits that behaviors typically occur due to a complex mixture of internal and external stimuli, coupled with years of conditioning that take place as a part of living life.

When it comes to dealing with mental issues, while some types of therapy are interested in getting to the deeper meaning of a particularly stubborn bit of mental clutter, CBT is only interested in getting results. It can be used in a wide variety of ways including as a means of creating new coping strategies for issues that have resisted other types of treatment. It can also effectively be used in either a group or a one-on-one scenario. Generally speaking, CBT lasts about 16 weeks on average.

CBT Stages

The goal of CBT is not to delve into every single issue you are experiencing in hopes of diagnosing yourself with an easy-to-classify illness. Instead, it is to get to the root of the issues that are causing the biggest problems in your life and to help you deal with them in a practical way. The goal can either be to find out what is causing maladaptive behaviors to manifest themselves or to change overall thought processes, both of which can be used to clear mental clutter successfully.

In order to get started, you are going to want to complete a CBT assessment, which contains five parts. First, you will need to determine the primary behaviors that are coming into play with your associated issue. Next, you will need to consider if these behaviors are either good or bad in the grand scheme of things before then considering the frequency, intensity, and duration of any negative behaviors. From there, you will then want to determine the most beneficial course of action you can embark on in order to correct any relevant negative behaviors. Finally, you will want to determine how effective the treatment is likely to be and plan ahead accordingly.

CBT Stage 1: Assessment – Creating a therapeutic alliance

While some individuals can find success on their own with a wide variety of different therapies, if you hope to use CBT to solve your issues you are going to need to be willing to speak with a therapist. What's more, you are going to need to form a therapeutic alliance with your therapist to ensure that you are able to generate real solutions to the problems you are hopping to deal with. This won't happen overnight, of course, and your first session will be spent getting to know one another so you can determine if you can form a productive relationship with this particular therapist. The therapist will also use this introductory session to determine your current emotional, physical, and mental state with the goal of getting to the root of your problems as quickly as possible.

CBT Stage 2: Cognitive – Harnessing and understanding your thoughts

After you have started a productive therapeutic alliance, it will then be time to get to the meat and potatoes of CBT. You will discuss your issues with your therapist who will, in turn, provide you with a roadmap for how to go about solving them. Generally speaking, this will start with taking a closer look at your thought processes and how they affect your daily life.

In order to do so, the first thing you will need to do is pay closer attention to the reasons you think the way you do, starting with any left over mental clutter that may be getting in the way. A discussion of leftover mental clutter is actually a common part of this step, regardless of what issues the client is looking to solve.

CBT believes that maladjusted thought patterns stem from specific unresolved issues in the past —mental clutter – which affects the way you currently act and think by creating what are known as schemas in your thought processes. Isolating your negative schemas and understanding how they affect you is likely to be a big part of your early CBT sessions.

CBT Stage 3: Behavioral – Improving your thought patterns and behaviors

After helping you to gain more active control over your thoughts, your therapist will then suggest new ways to develop positive thought patterns to replace those you have gotten rid of. Much of this stage is about practicing these new patterns until they become second nature. Regardless of how long this stage takes or what exercises your therapist prescribes, you will learn to strengthen and enhance the newer patterns that you have created. If the previous step was all about learning to control your thoughts, this step is all about controlling your actions. You will move on from this step when the new actions you have learned become habits themselves. This takes will generally take at least a month.

CBT Stage 4: Learning – Moving on and becoming your own therapist

The last part of CBT is learning to practice it effectively without the help of your therapist. This doesn't mean that you are going to be done with your treatment; it means that you will take control of your treatment and provide yourself with the structure you yourself need in order to move forward successfully. When it comes to using CBT to deal with mental clutter this means that you will not only be able to clear out existing clutter, but help prevent more from forming as well.

Chapter 8:
Minimalism

If you are like most people when you think of the concept of minimalism, you probably picture getting rid of absolutely everything you own, never buying anything new ever again and existing largely in a pure white room that is devoid of any life. While this may be true for some individuals, it is only because they feel happy taking things to extremes. In fact, a majority of minimalists get along just fine without resorting to anything remotely resembling such an austere state.

In fact, giving away all of their possessions, or even most of them, doesn't make someone a minimalist. Rather, doing so is often an expression of a new-found desire to be a minimalist as opposed to the cause. It is one aspect of the whole, but it is not the facet that you need to focus on in the moment. Instead, you could very well start with pairing down your mental clutter and find plenty of benefits as a result.

You see, what minimalism is truly about is taking a long hard look at your priorities with the goal of stripping away all the excess stuff, activities, thoughts, relationships, ideas, possessions, and whatever else it may be that doesn't actively add value to your life. If you can look at any facet of your life and say to yourself, with complete and utter certainty, "This is important to me", then minimalism says you should invest more time and effort into it. Otherwise, you should seriously consider cutting it out of your life completely.

The reason that material possessions are one of the first things to go for most minimalism enthusiasts is that when they stop and think about it these items are definitely not a crucial part of their lives. To experience this revelation for yourself, take 24 hours to really focus on the things in your life that are the most important to you: Odds are that the results will surprise you. If your day is full of things that don't make the short list, then a little minimalism in your life will likely do you good.

The following is a step-by-step guide to getting into a minimalism mindset.

Be accepting of the process

In order to transition into a minimalism lifestyle successfully, the first thing you are going to need to do is be accepting of the fact that you won't make your transition overnight. Once you come to terms with the fact that it is a process, you will naturally find it less infuriating when you don't start seeing results right off the bat. This mindset will also help you through the periods where nothing seems to be happening at all, and will also help you want to pack it all in and go back to your old ways. Keep in mind that wanting to change for the better and actually making that change are two very different things, but you will find it easier to keep the faith once you have adopted the process.

Understand why you are doing it

If you are coming to minimalism for the first time through this book, then determining your motivation should be easy as you are likely looking for a way to put your mental clutter in the dustbin once and for all. It is important to focus on this goal as a means of fully embracing the process of change that you are now undertaking. Not only will having a clear motivation in mind help you to always keep moving in the right direction, it will also ensure that the steps you take towards true minimalism are beneficial rather than just being a way to stimulate your life while you wait for the next hype train to jump onto.

Write it down

If you are having a hard time coming up with the proper motivation, you may find it useful to write down a list of all the reasons you want to embrace minimalism and then put them in order based on importance. Do you feel as though you don't get to spend enough time with your loved ones? Put it on the list. Do you feel as though you are so stressed financially that you can't sleep at night? Put it on the list. Feel as though mental clutter is making it difficult to get anything done no matter your best efforts? Maybe put that at the top of the list.

Create some new habits

After you have successfully identified your motivation, the next thing you are going to want to do is create a number of guiding principles to live by that also help to reinforce your motivation at the same time. When you are creating new habits, take the time to discard those that aren't working for you in the moment. For example, any habits that you already have that contributes to mental clutter, such as procrastinating, should be gotten rid of.

Once you have a few habits in place, you are going to want to go back and ask yourself what other habits could prove beneficial or what other habits are currently detrimental to your mental health. Keep doing this until you feel as though you have reached the true heart of your desire for minimalism. In getting to the heart of the matter, you are likely to find a number of rules and habits that come easily as a result. You may also find a desire to stop simply living in the world and start truly interacting with it.

It is important to keep an eye on these rules as they will help keep you motivated when the going gets tough. It is important to define what rules work for you and really own them: They are yours and they exist for the benefit of improving your life. This means not listening to anyone else when it comes to your rules, or adopting rules you don't need because society expects it of you.

With these details in mind, you should be able to start developing an outline of what your ideal minimalist life looks like. While it can be a lot of work, moving through this process and coming to your own conclusions is going to be far more beneficial than limiting your possessions to what someone else says a true minimalist should own.

Focus on improving your mindset

Once you have a number of new habits that you are solidifying, the next thing you will need to do is work on changing your overall mindset to ensure that you are supporting your new habits on all sides. This will look different for everyone based on the specific issues that they are working on, but the important thing is to emphasize your motivation and your habits throughout your day as much as possible. Keep in mind that you need to practice a new habit for 30 days before it sticks, so ensure that you have the time to devote to minimalism before you get started.

Don't try and change everything all at once

Making the decision to go all in on minimalism can be intimidating, especially if you feel as though you have a long way to go before you reach your goal. Luckily, you don't need to worry about making every change all at once, which is not only needlessly difficult but far more likely to end in disaster. Instead, you can start small and work up to the more lifechanging parts of your new plan. Use the following ideas to get started on the right foot.

- Pick one piece of mental clutter to tackle.

- Fill one trash bag full of clothes and donate it.

- Clean out your junk drawer.

- Break down your new habits into steps and take the first one of each.

- Create a few mantras that will help you stick to a minimalist mindset.

Get rid of duplicates

A great way to get started when it comes to paring down your property is to simply get rid of anything that you have multiples of. All you need to do is get a large box and walk through your home and whenever you find a duplicate of something that has no immediate use, put it in the box. Once you fill out the box, and odds are you will fill the box, you can then simply label it "Duplicates" and stick it somewhere out of mind for the next month.

After a month, anything that you didn't find a use for can be sold, donated or discarded as you have proved you have no need of it. Once you have gotten rid of the duplicates box, you can go back and fill it with anything you keep around "just in case". Repeat the process of getting rid of things every 30 days and then do it again and again until you have paired down your possessions to just the things you actually use. While this will likely mean making some hard choices from time to time, you will feel better when it is all said and done, guaranteed.

Label one area clutter free

Alternately, a good place to start is by declaring a specific part of your home to be clutter free. This can be a drawer, a countertop, or an entire room; any amount of space is fine as long as you stake your claim to it and keep it free of clutter. From there you can slowly expand outward until your entire home is a clutter free zone. This is one of few techniques that are very effective for converting households to minimalism. You can read more about it in my book – _Minimalism for Families: Live a Minimalist Life in a Minimalist Home with the Ones You Love_.

Take your time

As previously mentioned, living a minimalist lifestyle is a process, which means you need to give yourself the time it takes to adapt to the changes you are trying to make. None of this will happen overnight and if you find yourself getting frustrated, fighting back against the changes you are making or feeling impatient because you don't seem to be moving forward, will only lengthen the journey. As such, if you find yourself getting frustrated, take a step back and do something that is purposefully relaxing and don't think about decluttering for a few days. Instead, opt to clear some mental clutter for the time being. When you come back to decluttering your physical possessions with a clear mind, odds are you will feel refreshed and ready to tackle the change anew.

Don't wait to enjoy life

Odds are you aren't considering minimalism just as a means of simplifying your life, but you are doing it to take back your life in a more proactive way. Mental clutter and the other stressors of the modern world can make it easy to feel as though you are suffocating. Minimalism can certainly be a lifeline, but that doesn't mean you need to successfully transition to a minimalism lifestyle before you can start enjoying yourself again. True minimalism is about investing your time in an intentional manner and that should start as soon as possible.

Conclusion

Well, that's it; you've made it to the end of this book – *Declutter: Free Your Mind from Mental Clutter*. Hopefully you have learned about some of the ways that people just like you have successfully cleared their minds of mental clutter. Learning about the process and actually committing to it are two very different things, however, but committing to it is what you need to do if you hope to see a real change in your daily experiences.

Mental clutter could very well be dramatically decreasing your quality of life, but only you can say for sure. As such, it is time to stop reading and start actively taking your mental state into your own hands. Look through the symptoms discussed in the first chapter and see if they apply to your life. If they do, take steps to clear them up once and for all; and if they don't, do what you can to remain vigilant against them in the future. Remember, remaining free of mental clutter is a marathon, not a sprint. As such, slow and steady wins the race.

Mindfulness for Beginners

How Present Living Can Change Your Life

Addison Fenn

express written consent from the Publisher. All additional rights reserved.

The information in the following pages is broadly considered to be a truthful and accurate account of facts, and as such any inattention, use or misuse of the information in question by the reader will render any resulting actions solely under their purview. There are no scenarios in which the publisher or the original author of this work can be in any fashion deemed liable for any hardship or damages that may befall them after undertaking information described herein.

Additionally, the information in the following pages is intended only for informational purposes and should thus be thought of as universal. As befitting its nature, it is presented without assurance regarding its prolonged validity or interim quality. Trademarks that are mentioned are done without written consent and can in no way be considered an endorsement from the trademark holder.

Introduction

Congratulations for purchasing this book – *Mindfulness for Beginners: How Present Living Can Change Your Life* – and thank you for doing so. Whether you realize it or not, purchasing this book was the first step towards living more fully in the present while at the same time improving your physical and mental health in a wide variety of surprising ways.

In order to help you along the path to inner peace, the following chapters will discuss everything you need to know in order to get started practicing mindfulness, not just someplace quiet that is free of distractions, but at any point throughout the day regardless of where you are or what you are doing at the time. For starters, you will learn about the long history of mindfulness as well as the many reasons you should strongly consider adding it to your daily routine. Next, you will learn the basics of mindfulness through the practice of mindfulness mediation.

From there, you will learn about two variations of mindfulness that utilize a group therapy setting, mindfulness-based stress reduction and mindfulness-based cognitive therapy, to ensure that you have a broad spectrum of choices available to you when it comes to getting started on the right foot. Finally, you will learn about several alternative ways to practice mindfulness, including while you are in the middle of your daily commute, while at work or while at home doing a variety of everyday tasks.

There are plenty of books like this on the market, so thanks again for choosing this one! Every effort was made to ensure it is full of as much useful information as possible. Please enjoy!

Chapter 1:
Why Mindfulness?

Despite having been a part of religious rituals of all shapes and sizes for thousands of years via meditation, the concept of mindfulness has only gained traction in the Western world in the past 50 years. This boom in popularity is thanks in large part to mindfulness's well-documented ability to improve mental health via the treatment of anxiety, stress, drug addiction, and more. These benefits were first brought to light by a professor named Dr. Jon Kabat-Zinn in the 1970s when he published his findings linking mindfulness to stress reduction.

His findings led to a flurry of other studies on the practice, and then to a more in-depth understanding of the ways in which being mindful can improve a person's health by directly fighting off numerous common ailments. It's not just a hit among the naturopathic medicine crowd either; studies on its effectiveness have actually proven to be conclusive that mindfulness meditation is being used as a treatment for a host of conditions in places like veteran associations, hospitals, and even prisons.

At its heart, mindfulness is all about focusing your mind in such a way that you become more fully aware of each moment than you ever thought possible. Throughout your daily life, you are most likely in a constant state of thinking about the future and worrying about what is going to happen next – needing to do this and do that – when really you need to find a way to spend more time in the present. This, in turn, allows you to exist more completely in any given moment by expanding your consciousness to the fullest.

Now this may sound like a difficult request at first, and depending on your natural mindset it might very well be. Luckily, being mindful is a skill and like any other skill it can be improved upon if you practice it regularly. What's more, after you get the basics down, practicing mindfulness is as easy as finding a moment or two to focus on all of the information your senses are providing you with in the present. To start, however, you are going to need to plan on setting aside 15 minutes a day, every day, to dedicate to being completely mindful. If you can find this amount of time each day for a month, you will likely notice a decrease in your overall stress levels and an increase in your feeling of self.

That's not all as studies have shown that those who practice mindfulness regularly also find that they have an easier time freeing their minds from the types of negative thought patterns that they have previously found easy to become stuck in on a regular basis. Mindfulness is so effective at this task, that a study out of Johns Hopkins University recently found that it treats issues including attention deficit disorder, depression, and anxiety just as well as many of the medicines currently on the market today. Another recent study also showed students preparing to take the Graduate Records Examination, the most common test to obtain admission into graduate school, who practiced mindfulness meditation regularly prior to testing scored approximately 10 percent better than their less mindful peers.

Vipassana

With the wealth of mental and physical benefits mindfulness offers, is it any wonder that it is used daily by countless people all around the world? Mindfulness meditation, the most common entry point for most people into the habit of being mindful, has its roots in an ancient type of structured meditation known as vipassana – which roughly translated means a mental state that promotes living in the moment and understanding how the present becomes the future. Those who are able to successfully reach vipassana are said to have a greater understanding of the universe and their place in it.

In order to reach a state of vipassana, seekers aim to attain what are known as the three marks of existence – which are non-self, impermanence, and dissatisfaction – which when kept in harmony are said to bring unity to all living things. Non-self is the idea of understanding the boundaries between the physical world and the self. It is also the idea that understanding these boundaries makes it easier to understand the hidden meaning found in both the self and the physical world. Impermanence is the belief that nothing is permanent, whether good or bad, because change is inevitable. Dissatisfaction, meanwhile, refers to the innate desire everyone has to find satisfaction in the fleeting experiences of life and the feeling of loss when that satisfaction wanes. This, in turn, supports the idea that only by accepting all aspects of life as temporary can anyone really finds true happiness in experiences.

Physical benefits

The feelings of well-being that come along with practicing mindfulness aren't just emotional; they are caused by actual, physical changes to the brains of those who practice mindfulness on a regular basis. Neuroimaging scans show that those who are more mindful are actually able to process information more effectively, regulate emotions more easily, and remain focused on a single task for longer periods of time than those who do not practice mindfulness.

Related studies also found that those who have spent their lives practicing mindfulness typically have a brain that is heavier by volume than those who don't. As a brain's volume is a measure of its overall health, this added vitality can be seen to cause additional benefits as well. One place this increased vitality turns up is in the hippocampus, which means mindful individuals typically retain new information more effectively and with less effort. Being mindful regularly also suppresses activity in the amygdala which means mindfulness can also decreases the amount of anxiety, stress, and fear that you feel as a result. This process is also aided by the fact that being mindful reduces the amount of the stress-causing hormone, cortisol, which your body produces naturally.

In addition to the above specifics, mindfulness meditation appears to improve overall physical health. While admittedly anecdotal, those who regularly practice mindfulness report feeling sick less frequently and recover more quickly when they do fall ill. Whether this is actually a physical response to the process or a mental one that leads them to feel healthier than they actually are, remains unclear. However, my speculation is that the less stress you feel as a result of practicing mindfulness results in a stronger, healthier, and more efficient immune system and body. Regardless, mindfulness has many benefits with little to no risk involved. The only thing you need to be mindful is to be committed to being present.

Chapter 2:
Getting Started – Mindfulness Meditation

While the idea of looking inward to find a previously hidden well of tranquility and peace might sound either daunting or preposterous, the fact of the matter is that it is something that anyone can successfully master as long as they dedicate the time and mental energy required to ensure they practice being mindful each and every day. While this chapter will primarily concern itself with the practice of mindfulness meditation, rest assured that the tips and tricks you learn along the way will apply to the other types of mindfulness discussed in later chapters.

In fact, one of the best things about mindfulness meditation is how very malleable it is, which means that you should be able to easily fit it into your schedule no matter what. When you are first getting started, however, you are going to want to set aside a set time and location each day to practice as this repetition will help you pick up the habit more easily overall. The location you pick should be one that is free of extraneous distractions so that you can focus completely on the task at hand. Being mindful is all about creating space between the information your body is providing you with and your reactions to that information. This means the fewer stimuli you have to work with at first, the easier the process will be overall.

Start off on the right foot

Make a commitment: Studies show that it takes about 30 days for a new habit to become a permanent part of your daily routine, which means you will need to practice mindfulness meditation every day for the first month for the best results. Unfortunately, for many people, this is easier said than done as mindfulness meditation is extremely low impact and requires very little preparation, making it easy to find an excuse to push it out of schedule – especially if said individual is already extremely busy.

If you find yourself constantly coming up with excuses to get out of practicing mindfulness meditation, keep the following ancient proverb in mind: "Practice mindfulness meditation for fifteen minutes every day unless, of course, you are extremely busy in which case you should practice for thirty minutes instead". Don't let external forces dictate your path to personal improvement, create a meditation schedule that you can stick with every day and commit to the practice for 30 days. If feel like you are not seeing any results, at least you can say you gave it a fair chance. The odds are good, however, that you won't want to go back.

Focus on the moment: While your end goal should be to find a state of internal calm, regardless of what is going on in the world around you, it is difficult for most people to reach this state right away. Rather, they find it easier to start quieting their thoughts by focusing all of their attention on the signals that their bodies are relaying to them in the moment.

While, at first, you may not feel as though you are processing too much data from the world around you, especially if you are practicing in a quiet, calm space as suggested, this could not be further from the truth. The fact of the matter is that most of the time your brain filters out around 80 percent of the information it receives on any given day – which means that information is there: You just need to get in the habit of accessing it regularly.

Over time, you will learn to tune out the thoughts you have regarding your everyday routines, and instead tap directly into whatever it is that is going on around you. It is important to process the information that your senses are providing you while, at the same time, making a conscious effort to not pass judgement or dig too deeply into anything that crosses your mind. Judging results in additional thoughts in one way or another. And in turn, this creates even more thoughts. This accumulation of more and more thoughts will make it practically impossible for you to focus on the task at hand.

Remember, when it comes to mindfulness meditation the goal is to get as close to the moment as possible, which means ignoring everything else that is going on with the exception of what your senses are providing you. To reach this state, you will start by focusing on your breathing, especially on the way the air feels as it enters and exits your lungs. Also focus on the way the air smells and tastes.

Once you have narrowed your focus to only this band of information, the next thing you are going to want to do is to start expanding your observations to include the other sensations your body might be experiencing. With the top level of your mind temporarily cleared of your immediate thoughts, you can then focus on going deeper into yourself in search of the point where your mind is content not creating any new thoughts and simply exists in a relaxed, peaceful state.

Avoid your thoughts: When you first begin practicing mindfulness, it is perfectly natural for your mind to constantly fill with thoughts. This typically occurs because you have trained yourself over the years, whether you realize it or not, to constantly move from one thought to the next, in hopes of solving the latest major crisis. This is, of course, the polar opposite of what you are striving for with mindfulness – which is why it is only natural for you to expect a bit of an adjustment period.

When you find these types of thoughts breaching your quest for inner peace, it is important to avoid interacting with them and instead simply let them float away. Likewise, if you realize that you have started to interact with one of these thoughts, it is important that you let go of it without feeling angry with yourself for letting it slip in or feeling guilty for interacting with it. The fact of the matter is that any additional thought after the first does little good and only compounds the problem further.

While this can be a very difficult step for many people to master, it is important to remain stalwart in your convictions and avoid stray thoughts wherever you find them until it becomes second nature for you to do so. When it comes to clearing your mind as thoroughly as possible, you may find it helpful to visualize the thoughts that typically flow through your head as being incased in a bubble floating by. If you get trapped by one of the bubbles simply picture it popping or floating away to get yourself back on track. It seems silly but this is what personally helped me, so give it a try!

Keep it up: While early on in the process you may start to lose focus after a few minutes, it is important to keep pushing yourself to remain in a state of mindfulness for as long as possible each and every day. This is especially true if you find your mind wandering as you should be able to correct that habit the more you have to deal with it.

Trying to reach a state of mindfulness can be especially difficult if you have not yet reached an ideal, quiet state of mind. To understand the type of mindset you are striving to achieve, consider the period of blankness that you experience after you have been asked a question but before your mind registers a response. Finding a way to reach this type of state is key to your long-term success.

What happens next?

While there are plenty of proven positive side effects of practicing mindfulness, most of them are difficult to track on your own without specialized equipment as they occur at a biological level you can't see or occur on a mental level which is difficult to observe without bias. Instead, you will likely know that you are on the right track when you start to see changes in the mental conditioning you have been living with your entire life.

Modern society often instills in individuals a desire to hide their flaws and to treat any uncomfortable feelings or thoughts they have in much the same way. Over time, this leads to a desire to revise the truth and rewrite history, so it shows things in a more positive light overall. Despite not being an especially healthy way to deal with existing issues, this common habit actually stems from the well-known flight or fight reflex that has helped humanity's ancestors survive against threats regardless if they were real or imagined.

This impulse helped your ancient ancestors survive, and even thrive, amongst the harsh conditions they lived with day to day. But these days, if this impulse is left unchecked, it can instead easily lead to a scenario where it undermines the qualities and traits that make you unique. This, in turn, leads to one of the greatest benefits of mindfulness: It provides those who practice it with a greater understanding of themselves, which is the first step to a greater acceptance of their strengths and weaknesses and the ways the two can be used together for the best results.

Regularly practicing mindfulness and sticking with it in the long-term can replace this negative mindset with one that is much more positive, which is referred to as radical acceptance. Simply put, radical acceptance allows you to more easily get in touch with the things you are experiencing or feeling in the moment, without having to worry about societal filters getting in the way.

Radical acceptance makes it easier for those who are deeply connected to past negative experiences to understand that the experience doesn't have to define them and has no bearing on the quality of a person they are as a whole. For those who are dealing with these types of issues, coming to this conclusion can be a truly freeing experience that is difficult to top.

A major part of mindfulness and radical acceptance is embracing the idea that all of your firsthand experiences happened the way they really did – and not in an idealized fashion. This kind of perspective leads to a greater overall tolerance for negative experiences as a whole, which should make it easier for these experiences to occur without damaging your mental state.

The improved mental state that comes along with learning to be more mindful also comes with the natural side effect of learning to be less judgmental, not just of your experiences but your thoughts as well. Cultivating a habit of remaining mindful means suspending your inner critic and take a more product look at your reactions, feeling, and thoughts and why they make you feel the way you do.

Finally, you should find that regularly practicing mindfulness will naturally improve your ability to be aware of what is going on around you at all times, even when you are preoccupied with problems or thoughts. Generally speaking, most people are so focused on the mistakes they have already made, or those they might make in the future, that they let the present pass them by without a second thought. This can be a difficult problem to avoid as it can be easy to miss the pleasures of the present without actually realizing what is going on.

Instead of existing in this mental twilight state, spending more time truly in the present will help you improve your total situational awareness which means you will have a better idea of what is going on around you at all times. This, in turn, allows you to more accurately measure your experiences to determine how they are affecting your sense of self without the baggage that such things typically carry around with them. Essentially, meta-awareness allows you to view yourself in a detached and objective manner which can benefit virtually every aspect of your life.

Chapter 3:
Mindfulness-Based Stress Reduction

Mindfulness-based stress reduction (MBSR) is a type of group treatment used to assist those with a wide variety of issues that, for one reason or another, are difficult to treat in a more traditional setting. MBSR was first introduced by Dr. Kabat-Zinn, soon after releasing his initial findings on mindfulness as a whole. Since its introduction in the 1970s, it has gone on to be used in hospitals around the world.

For those who are interested in becoming a certified MBSR teacher, the University of Massachusetts Medical Center offers a seven-day course on the practice. This course has certified more than 1,000 MBSR instructors who are now operating in more than 30 different countries around the world. Major corporations, like General Motors, even have an MBSR specialist on staff to aid high-level employees in their meditative practices.

MBSR practices

The average MBSR program lasts for about eight weeks and includes weekly two-hour sessions as well as a one-day retreat that focuses on helping participants maintain a state of mindfulness for a full six hours. The program also includes a variety of homework exercises that participants are supposed to work through on their own, which lasts roughly an hour, everyday. These exercises are a blend of yoga, various mindfulness practices, and a process known as body scanning.

Body scanning: Body scanning is the first formal technique that is taught during the early days of the workshop. Essentially it involves lying flat on your back and focusing all of your attention to various regions of the body, starting with your toes and moving all the way to the top of the head. During this period new MBSR practitioners learn the core tenants of the process which include not being judgmental, not seeking acceptance from others, not holding onto the past, trust, patience, and mindfulness.

Focused mindfulness: Focused mindfulness is a common MBSR exercise that functions largely the same as traditional mindfulness meditation with an increased focus on looking inward to consider what is actively going on in your mind. This is useful for those who have deep-seated issues that they have been unable to shake, as it allows them to see where their issues are still cropping up and causing trouble in their day to day lives. For example, if you respond to nagging or criticism from others with rage, consider why you feel the way you do. Oftentimes, you yourself are frustrated with your own actions or inactions too. You don't mean any harm when you reply with anger or rage; instead, focused mindfulness may help you realize that it is you are at your tipping point and that you are crying for help.

Awareness mindfulness: While focused mindfulness allows you to look at the state of your mind from within it, awareness mindfulness allows you to look at your mind as if it belonged to someone else. The goal of this exercise is to look at your primary thoughts and assumptions as if they belonged to someone else for the purpose of determining if they are as rational as you likely assume they are. Looking at the things you hold most dearly to be true without the trappings of history and emotion you typically hang them on can be a great way to cut dead weight that is keeping you from truly being your best.

Switching between focused and awareness mindfulness: When it comes to switching between focused mindfulness and awareness mindfulness the best way to get started is to visualize your thoughts as a stream of bubbles, and then choose one of them to maintain your focus on while the shift occurs. Doing so will give you a touchstone, or guidepost, that you can use as you transition your thoughts to find your footing with the new way of thinking. Ideally, the touchstone you choose should be a vivid thought or memory, anything that you won't have difficulty looking at from all angles. Once you have used your touchstone to attune yourself to your current way of thinking, you can then expand your analysis from there.

Object meditation: As the name suggests in this exercise you practice mindfulness meditation, only instead of focusing on the sensations that your body is providing to you – you focus on either an item that is a part of the space you are in or one you carry with you expressly to aid in your journey to mindfulness. Regardless, if you have difficulty with traditional mindfulness meditation then you may find greater success with a physical item to focus on instead. Don't be afraid to manipulate the object in your hands while completing this exercise; the sense of touch is exceedingly powerful, and you could easily find a mindful state by considering the physical aspects of an object alone.

MBSR Takeaways

Although mindfulness-based stress reduction is usually handled in group settings, there are many strategies and techniques that you can take away from it without going through the course. The most useful of which are focused mindfulness and awareness mindfulness because they can be done anywhere and at any time.

Focused mindfulness detaches you from your sense of being: It addresses why you may feel or think something by removing you from your emotions and thoughts. For example, if you have hatred towards wealthy individuals, you may have a negative relationship with money because you grew up poor: Growing up, your family and environment ingrained in you the belief that the accumulation of wealth is bad, thus creating your current feelings of hatred for wealthy individuals today.

Awareness mindfulness helps you realize whether how you think or feel is skewed towards your biases, which are obtained through your particular experiences in life. For example, continuing from above, having grown up poor you may believe that you are less privileged and that the world is unjust. However, if you project that belief onto an individual like Gary Vaynerchuk, who believes that poverty is what shaped him into who he is today, you may realize that having grown up poor is a blessing in disguise – it does not dictate whether you succeed in life or not.

Of course, body scanning and object meditation are useful tools too. However, for beginners such as you who may not be willing to commit to the physical aspects of meditating, focused mindfulness and awareness mindfulness are the real gems of mindfulness-based stress reduction.

Chapter 4:
Mindfulness-Based Cognitive Therapy

Mindfulness-based cognitive therapy (MBCT) is a variation of mindfulness that was developed by several researchers around the turn of the century. MBCT is based around the idea that the human mind possesses two distinct modes when it comes to utilizing data, one for receiving information and another for processing the data it has received. It generally takes the form of an eight-week course that is designed to help participants deal with a wide variety of physical and mental health issues.

Another major part of the process is what is known as the interactive cognitive subsystems model. This model suggests that the human mind operates in both a being mode and a doing mode with a person who is mentally healthy being able to move between the two modes easily. With MBCT, the being mode is said to promote long-lasting emotional change, which is why it receives the greater amount of focus of the two.

Understanding MBCT

During an MBCT therapy session, participants learn to use a variety of cognitive methods in conjunction with mindfulness mediation as a means of short-circuiting the automatic thought processes they are having a hard time removing. Even if the situation that often leads to the issue passes, it is possible for additional, smaller negative stimuli to trigger more pronounced downward spirals after.

MBCT makes it possible for participants to learn to see themselves as separate from their moods and thoughts as a means of subjectively determining their current emotional state. It promotes the idea that while emotions and their current mental state can exist at the same time, there is no reason for one to affect the other in a serious way. Once this level of understanding is reached, it then becomes much more manageable for them to interject positive thoughts to banish negative moods.

Chapter 4: Mindfulness-Based Cognitive Therapy

MBCT techniques

MBCT is typically best conducted in a series of eight weekly group sessions. Each session tends to last about two hours, though participants will be required to complete homework exercises the other days of the week. These exercises include a variety of techniques to improve mindfulness as well as a series of audio recordings designed to aid in the process as well.

Three-minute breathing space: One unique exercise is known as the three-minute breathing space. This practice is broken into three steps, the first of which is to place yourself in a lightly mindful state where you can be aware of your thoughts without directly interacting with them. Once you have found this space, you will then want to narrow the total focus of your attention to just the breath entering and leaving the body. Hold this state where you focus on breathing only for three minutes before widening your focus once more.

Bringing the focus of your meditation down to just your breathing will teach you to tighten your focus beyond what regular mindfulness practices, cutting out everything except what is happening in the absolute moment. Honing in on and controlling your breathing has profound benefits, and can alter your mental state from a chaotic one to one that is serene.

Grounding: When a person experiences physical trauma, it impacts the brain as well as the body. This is why different people respond to the trauma they have previously experienced in different ways, as everyone is going to have different triggers. As it can be difficult to predict when a new trigger is going to materialize, a grounding exercise can be useful to help regain your sense of calm in the moment by pulling you out of the remembered experience and firmly grounding you in the here and now.

The most common and infamous way to ground yourself is through, lo and behold, breathing. Breathing is not only powerful – being able to control your mood, thoughts, and actions – but it can be done anywhere. Other grounding techniques exist, however, and they include:

- Letting the information from your senses in and describing your surroundings aloud in detail.

- Making a list of topics in a specific category such as television shows or foods you don't like.

- Preparing a coping statement ahead of time that reminds you that you are in the present and the feeling will pass. Say it to yourself frequently, even if you are feeling fine so that it becomes familiar. Doing so will help remind you of the situation when you start to lose control.

- Dig your heels into the ground as hard as you can. Use the resulting stimulation to remind yourself of where you are in the present and that you are still connected to the world around you. Think of it as literally grounding yourself like how you would use a grounding wire – to transfer any dangerous and negative thoughts and feelings to the earth.

- Carry a grounding object with you at all times. When you are feeling particularly grounded, hold the object in your hands and do your best to consciously associate it with your grounded state. Then, when you are having a particularly rough time, you can hold the object and use it to call upon your grounded state to pull you back to the present.

Mountain meditation: This variation of mindfulness mediation starts in the traditional way, by reaching a basic sense of mindfulness. Once you are in tune with what your senses are telling you, the next thing you are going to do is to picture the most majestic mountain you have ever seen. Continue concentrating on it and let it come into greater and greater focus. Visualize its lofty peaks, its mammoth base and visualize how it extends deep into the earth.

Once you feel as if you could reach out and touch the mountain, the next thing you are going to want to do is to become the mountain. Picture yourself as you are currently sitting and then picture the mountain overlapping you in your mind's eye. Share its massiveness, share its sense of majesty, become the mountain. Let your sense of time fade away as the seasons pass in the blink of an eye, snow comes and goes, plants grow, die and are reborn five times, then 10, then 100.

As the mountain, understand that none of this matters and that you are eternal. Life may come and go but you, the mountain will remain as you are until the sun burns from the sky and, even then, you will sit in eternal darkness. Eventually, you will want to separate from the mountain and become yourself again, slowly waking, slowly moving, but taking with you the feeling of supreme solitude and strength back into the real world.

MBCT Takeaways

Like mindfulness-based stress reduction, you don't have to undergo a session of mindfulness-based cognitive therapy in order to apply its practices in daily life. If you take a look at the three mindfulness-based cognitive therapy techniques listed above – breathing, grounding, and mountain meditation – you will notice that all three have something in common: They teach you how to handle undesirable situations.

Breathing and grounding are ways for you to control your mood and emotions, both of which dictate your actions. This can be extremely beneficial when you are stressed, anxious, or extremely upset. It can be easy to throw a tantrum when you are at your limit, but proper breathing and grounding can bring you to a state of mindfulness, peace, and tranquility instead.

Mountain meditation can be explained in one sentence: Nothing matters. Regardless of the incident or trauma you have been through, or will go through, it is nothing in the grand scheme of things. Suffered the loss of a loved one? Realize that death is a *not* a matter of "if", but of "when". Going through distress and don't know what to do about it? Like a mountain, do nothing: Change is inevitable and things will get better themselves – there is no need to stress about it. Realize that you may have gone through worse and that every time you were down you eventually got back up. Grew up with domestic violence? Acknowledge it but realize that nothing can be done about the past. And if you can't change the past, why worry about it today?

If you are interested in cognitive therapy or techniques like mindfulness-based cognitive therapy, consider checking out another book of mine – _Declutter: Free Your Mind from Mental Clutter_ – which explores concepts like neuro-linguistic programming and minimalism as tools for mindfulness.

Chapter 5:
Commuting Mindfully

The remainder of this book focuses on aspects of life where you can practice being mindful – such as when commuting. Although it does not specify the use of mindfulness-based stress reduction or mindfulness-based cognitive therapy techniques, feel free to implement them as needed.

Statistically speaking, odds are you spend more than an hour commuting to and from work each and every day. Most people fill this time by catching up on their paperwork, sneaking a quick bite to eat, or by cursing at those around them as they sit stuck in traffic. While these all things certainly help pass the time, practicing mindfulness during this part of your day has the potential to be a much more productive use of everyone's time. While it may seem surprising, the repetitive nature of this drive or commute actually makes it a great time to work on clearing your mind and achieving a state of mindfulness. This state of mindfulness then ensures that when you get where you are going, you will take a new and improved mental state with you.

By practicing mindfulness while driving or commuting via public transit, you will find that you are ready to start your workday by tackling your problems head on. And by the time you get home at the end of the day, you would have left your problems somewhere on the highway. Being mindful on the go will allow you to maintain a calm, focused state more regularly, while also ensuring that the natural stress of rush hour fades into the background so you remain a safe and courteous driver as well. In fact, it will actually make you a better driver as you will be completely focused on the moment and those that are sharing the road with you.

Steps to follow

In order to ensure each commute is as effective as possible, the first thing you will want to do is announce your intentions for this session of mindfulness as soon as you get into your vehicle. Saying it aloud connects you to the process more directly than if you were to just think it: It creates the impression that you will be held responsible by someone, somewhere, so it is important not to skip this step just because you are alone. Once you have clearly stated your intentions, the next thing you are going to want to do before starting your vehicle is to take five deep, controlled breaths. Doing so will allow you to focus on the sensations that your senses are providing you in the moment to ensure that you are ready to maintain a sense of mindfulness once you are on the road.

While doing so, consider the way your body feels sitting in your seat, the way the wheel feels beneath your palms, and the way the world looks in comparison to the way it usually looks. Oftentimes, individuals are amazed by the view of the city skyline at night in movies and the like, but don't realize that they get a similar view every time they drive on the highway at night. The view is there, but the perspective is not: We are so busy with our tasks we fail to acknowledge the beauty around us. Picking up steam from there, you are going to want to let your focus spread outward so that you feel your feet as they push the pedals.

As you start your commute, you are going to want to pay special attention to the many things that are going on around you. Consider the vehicles that are directly in your path, those moving in lanes that you can barely see, people walking on the sidewalk, and the planes flying above in the sky. Consider all the various buildings and signs you pass, ostensibly every day, and marvel at the fact that you have never seen them before. In addition to all of the information your eyes are providing you, make sure you also pay attention to the data your ears are providing as they convey the sounds of hundreds, if not thousands, of people all moving at once.

While it may strike you as too simple to be truly effective focusing on these things, and only these things, on your way to and from work should be enough to trigger the state of mindfulness that you are looking for. As the work day is typically the busiest time of day for most people, it will be perfectly natural for a stream of thoughts to be running through your head during this time – even if you have already mastered the practice of being mindful without distractions. Be resolute in your use of the methods discussed in the preceding chapter for dealing with them, and you will find the peace that you are looking for with practice.

Tips for improving your commute

Unplug from being mentally at work early: If you find that clearing your mind during your morning commute is especially difficult, then it could be that you are plugging into your work environment too early in the day. As such, if you are having a hard time focusing on the moment during your morning commute you may want to make a conscious effort to avoid checking your email or social media for the purpose of engaging with work before you set foot on the premises. While you will likely find it difficult to ignore all of your notifications at first, once you break the habit you will likely find that your mornings are much more relaxing as a result.

Prepare ahead of time: If you find that you have a difficult time reaching a state of mindfulness once you are in your vehicle, you may find it helpful to do a sort of self-assessment before you reach your vehicle. Run through a list of things that may affect or have affected your day before. Reaching out for a state of mindfulness afterwards will then allow you to get all of those thoughts related to out of your head beforehand so that they will be less likely to intrude later on.

Supercharge your mindfulness experience: To ensure you get as much out of each commute as possible, you can use every moment that you are forced to stop to close your eyes, breathe deeply, and refocus on your mindful state. The constant stop-and-go of gridlock traffic creates a natural barrier for thoughts, giving you a natural point to reattune yourself to the process. This is also a good opportunity to refocus your attention on what your senses are telling you to the exclusion of all other thought.

Chapter 6:
Finding Mindfulness at Work

The combination of increased responsibility and a general decrease in the level of control over one's life makes the workday the most stressful part of the day for most people, and with good reason. This perfect storm of stress naturally leads to increased levels of anxiety and tension, generally without any hope of relief in sight. However, you can flip the script on this daily occurrence by discreetly making mindfulness a part of your daily workplace routine.

Practicing mindfulness in the workplace will not only decrease stress and anxiety, but it can also make it easier for you to focus on a particularly difficult project or help you find the solution to the problem you have been stuck on for weeks. Being mindful at work does this by making it easier for you to think outside the box. While not everyone will be able to take advantage of mindfulness practices at work, with a little bit of practice most people should be able to find some time to squeeze a little bit of mindfulness in between their other tasks.

While, individually, the amount of benefit that each one of these micro-mindfulness exercises provides is minimal the effects are cumulative – which means that the end result will ultimately lead to a sense of inner peace that is greater than the sum of its parts. While it might seem difficult to juggle the demands of the day, the demands of your coworkers and everything else that life throws at you, you can consider each micro mindfulness session as an island of calm in an otherwise choppy sea.

Getting started

Mindfulness in the workplace should be used as a tool for the purpose of squeezing out every last bit of efficiency from the day that you can. Do this by thinking about how you can use your time as productively as possible during each micro mindfulness session. If you are already using your commute to practice mindfulness, then when you arrive at work you will already be in a mindful state that will allow you to get the most out of each moment. In order to keep the mindfulness train rolling, you will want to take a moment or two between tasks in order to focus on your breathing and thus the sensory data that your body is providing.

This doesn't need to be the sort of elaborate process that you learned to complete at home; it should only take a minute or two to ensure your head remains on straight throughout the day. Quantity trumps quality in this situation and if you practice each time you switch tasks you will find that your early-morning mindfulness state persists throughout the day. This is not to say that you fail if you can't take a moment to be mindful between every set of tasks though. As long as you fit in some sessions of mindful thinking whenever and wherever you can you will come out miles ahead in the long-term.

For many people, clearing their mind during the work day can be extremely difficult. If your job leaves you little time to sneak in a bit of mindfulness, simply start with whatever you can get – even if it is just 30 seconds. Over time, you will get a feel for the solace and figure out the best ways to chain dozens, if not hundreds, of mindfulness sessions together throughout the day.

Micro-mindfulness options

Focus on your fingers: If you work an office job, then one of the easiest ways to sneak in a bit of mindfulness is to spend some time focusing on the way your fingers move as they glide across the keyboard. You can focus on the rhythmic sound the keys make as they are pressed, and if you focus hard enough you can pick out the individual sensations of each keypress as it happens. Take some time to consider the way in which your mind forms words before your fingertips tap them out. Consider the connection between the body and the mind that is at play and the ways in which you typically take it all for granted.

Watch your posture: If you spend most of your day in an office chair, then focusing on your posture is another good way to sneak in a bit of mindfulness. You can begin by relaxing your entire body, beginning with your neck and working all the way down to the tips of your toes. After you have relaxed, you will then be able to more clearly focus on the signals being provided by your body in an effort to locate any pain points. Once these points have been identified, you can then adjust your posture until you are completely free of pain and so that you can refocus on the task at hand.

Respond slower: If much of your day consists of responding to the requests of others, either via email or over the phone, then a great way to throw in some extra mindfulness is to simply take 30 seconds between each request to re-center yourself and practice being mindful in a microburst. This has the added benefit of helping you clear your mental state before conversing with others. While 30 seconds might not seem like much, it can actually add up quite quickly. For example, if you deal with 70 requests that require your response per day you are actually spending 35 minutes of your day being mindful. Give it a try; you will be surprised at how much extra mindfulness you can sneak in on an average day.

Look for opportunities for repetition: Any scenario that requires routine or repetition is always a great opportunity for practicing mindfulness. The best activities are those that combine basic physical activity with the freedom to focus exclusively on the task at hand as they are essentially a free pass to practice mindfulness. To do so successfully, all you need to do is focus on the task to the exclusion of all else, and you should be able to easily fill your head with mindful thoughts.

Focus on your coworkers: If your days are spent constantly interacting with your coworkers, then you can find an opportunity to be mindful by devoting all of your mental focus to listening to whatever it is that they have to say. While this is not to say that the insights from your coworkers are all going to be winners or optimistic, but focusing the full scope of your attention on them can allow you to find a state of mindfulness that will also make them feel as though you are really committed to hearing them out.

Prepare for your end of the day commute: In order to maximize the effectiveness of your time spent being mindful on your commute home, you should try and use the last few minutes of your workday to wrap things up as much as possible and then compartmentalize everything so that nothing follows you home. Take some time to think about all of the things you have already accomplished, reflect on your various failures and successes, and how they fit into the big picture. Once you have finished reflecting, mentally close the door on the workday with the understanding that any leftover problems don't need to be solved until tomorrow. You will find that doing so makes your evening mindfulness session even more effective than it might otherwise be. Above all, repeat the mantra that tomorrow is another day and another opportunity to get everything right.

Notice the benefits of mindfulness at work: While you may feel that taking the time out of your day to be mindful at work causes you to work more slowly, the reality is that the opposite is true. In fact, the more hectic your job is the more you likely spend time reacting to things without thinking them through fully. Once you start being more mindful, however, you will find that your mind is clear enough to stop reacting to things in the moment and is instead able to proactively respond to situations in a productive manner.

With enough time spent practicing mindfulness at work, you will likely find it easier to come up with new approaches to problems both new and old. This is only going to be the case, however, if you stop thinking about the situations you find yourself in as problems and start thinking about them as challenges to be overcome. Problems are simply roadblocks to success while challenges, on the other hand, are incidents that can be learned from and bested for the betterment of you and your place of business. When you come across a challenge that has you stumped, consider writing it down and focusing on it completely to the exclusion of everything else. If you have been practicing mindfulness regularly you will be surprised at how quickly a previously unthought of solution may reveal itself.

Chapter 7:
Remaining Mindful at Home

When it comes to practicing mindfulness throughout your day, there is no easier place to do so than in your very own home as it is there that you will have the greatest overall control of your surroundings. In fact, after you have developed a habit of practicing mindfulness you will find that there is little you can do that doesn't lend itself to the practice. What follows is a list of activities you can use as an excuse to be mindful, some of which are sure to surprise you.

Do chores mindfully: Before you started to look at the world through mindful lens, odds are one of your least favorite things to do are household chores as they tend to involve nothing but boring menial labor. Moving forward, however, if you look at them with an eye towards mindfulness you will find that they are not only a great way to be productive physically, but mentally as well. Don't forget, any activity with a physical component that doesn't require active attention is a potential outlet for your mindfulness as long as you approach it properly.

When it comes to tackling your chores, before you dive in you are going to want to take some time to clear your mind and to enter a simple, mindful state where you are in tune with the signals your body is sending out and taking in. Once you have primed your mind, you will then want to attack the activity in question with a vengeance, existing in the moment of the activity to the point where the outside world simply fades away.

To keep your thoughts in check, consider the way your hands feel as they go through the motions of the activities you are completing. Focus on the details your eyes provide you with as you alter the physical world in front of you for the better. Focus on the smells that accompany the task and the productivity they signify. Then, once you have finished, be sure to actively take another moment to savor the feeling of accomplishment that comes with a job well done. Ideally, you will want to take care of any of the preparation that your chores are going to require beforehand so that you can go from one task to another without breaking your mindful state. With a little practice, this can easily extend how long you are in a state of mindfulness to an hour or more.

Bathe mindfully: It doesn't matter if you typically bathe in the morning or in the evening, this time can easily be used to either help prepare you for your day or to help you decompress at the end of a long day with the simple addition of mindfulness. While most people rush through their daily bathing routine and don't give the activity any real thought, bathing is actually full of potentially mindful experiences that you can take advantage.

First and foremost, the isolating nature of the experience provides a natural barrier to the problems of the day. Maximize this isolation as much as possible. Draw a line in your mind between the bathroom and the outside world and don't let any stray thoughts cross it, no matter what. Before you commence your bathing ritual, you will want to center yourself and enter the early stages of a mindful state.

Once you are ready focus on the feeling of the water on your skin, the way the water feels as it engulfs your body, and the temperature change that comes along with it. Use the various repetitive tasks at your disposal to add additional sensations to the experience and, as you move through them let your mind reach a state of mindfulness. This is also the scenario where you are likely to get the most use out of your sense of smell by focusing on the scents that surround you, which is a powerful way to fight back against any thoughts that might attempt to intrude.

Exercising mindfully: Any activity that doesn't require your full, active attention is a great candidate for mindfulness. Exercise is no exception. In fact, exercise and mindfulness is an extremely effective pair as exercise naturally pushes the sensations the body is providing to the forefront of the mind, making mindfulness only an additional step away. As such, it doesn't require much more to move into a truly mindful state. And in a way, you strengthen both your body and mind all at the same time. What's more, those who make a habit of exercising while practicing mindfulness report a noticeable increase in their overall level of endurance. As such, being mindful and in the present nets you a performance boost as well.

In order to ensure your period of exercise is as mindful as possible, you are going to need to stop focusing on getting everything right and instead trust your body to take care of the actions itself. Focus on the individual body parts in question, the way they feel as they complete their repetitions and the myriad of additional sensations they are providing you with while you put them through their paces. Each time you complete an exercise and prepare to move onto the next you can use the time to transition to refocus your attention on the moment and discard any thoughts that may have temporarily stolen your focus.

Being focused on the moment is no excuse to lose track of what you are doing, of course, as it can be easy to accidentally push yourself too hard and cause serious damage as a result. With that being said, the type of exercise you choose to pursue doesn't matter as long as it is one that you are already familiar with. When approaching a different exercise, consider getting into a rhythm before switching to mindfulness mode to prevent injuries.

Use social media mindfully: While the idea of interacting with social media while being mindful might sound absurd at face value, it isn't as far-fetched as you might expect; this is assuming you come at it with the right goal in mind, of course. While checking your latest notification can often draw you out of the moment and away from other mindfulness exercises, using social media with a purpose can actually improve your mindful state.

In order for this mindfulness exercise to work properly, the first thing you are going to need to do is to ensure you are in a space that is largely free of distractions so that you have nothing to distract yourself from the pictures you will soon be considering. This is an important step and is worth repeating as 85 percent of all social media usage takes place as a result of some type of multitasking. Remember, this is a mindfulness exercise, not an excuse to see what your favorite celebrities are doing on Instagram.

With these distractions out of the way, you will first want to ensure you prepare yourself by easing into a mindful state. Once you have the proper mindset queued up, you are going to want to look through a record of all of your texts or pictures and do your best to relive these moments as vividly as possible. Try and remember the exact feeling you had at the time and really let the memory consume you. Remember the signals that your body was providing at the time; consider the temperature, the people you were with, the sights, the smells, and the sounds. While it may take some practice, eventually you will be able to block out the outside world completely and exist solely in your memory.

Reflect on the day: If you have difficulty sleeping, you may find it helpful to work through a mindfulness exercise before bed. Doing so will allow you to offload the stress from the day either through taking a mental inventory or by physically writing all of your cares down on a piece of paper. As you might expect, you will want to prepare yourself before you get started for the best results. When you are ready to recount your day, you may find the tactile experience of writing in a journal makes it easier for you to tie yourself to the moment as you reflect.

For each entry you are going to want to go through the major beats of your day, taking special care to remember the sensations that went along with each. Be as descriptive as possible, especially with the negative experiences as this will help you draw out the sensations you don't want to remember and store them somewhere they won't be able to affect your sleep. With practice, this detailed examination of your day will make it easier for you to pick out various sensations that you might have missed while practicing other forms of mindfulness as well.

Budgeting mindfully: Being mindful also means being aware. And budgeting may be one of the best ways to be aware of what you consume and where it comes from because it covers many aspects of life.

Where you spend your cash can determine a lot about who you are. If you are very materialistic, you can see it in your expenses. If you are vegan, you are likely able to tell just by looking at your grocery list. If you are an entrepreneur or business owner, you can expect to see fluctuations in your cash flow.

If you don't have a budget, consider making one. Just thinking about your cash flow can help you become a lot more mindful about whom you are as a person. Budgeting is, in a way, a practical application of mindfulness in your everyday life. Consider my book on budgeting – titled *Minimalist Budget: Spend Less and Live More with a Minimalist Lifestyle* – if you need a place to start.

Start your day the right way: It doesn't matter in what way you start the day. As long as you have a morning routine you can use this exercise to ensure your day starts with an extra dose of mindfulness. When done properly, you can use the experiences you feel during this time to pull you even more fully into the moment to ensure your entire day is as mindful as possible. As this could be the only peaceful moment in an otherwise hectic day, it is best to make it count.

For starters, you should try and wake up in a mindful state. You can do so the moment you wake up by considering the thoughts in your head without directly interacting with them. Make an effort to continue with this mindset for as long as possible before you make your breakfast.

While preparing your first meal, you are going to want to focus on the anticipation of the act. Consider the way your hands feel as they go through the familiar motions, and the other sensations that go along with the act of creation. Once you have finished, it is now time to sit quietly and focus on what you have made. Take an extra moment to consider the way it looks and smells before finally finding out how it tastes.

As you consume your meal consider the way it makes you feel and the benefits it is providing your body. Focus on these thoughts, and only these thoughts, as you finish the meal. If you find your mind wandering to the thoughts of the day, gently pull it back on track. Once you are done, look at what is left on your plate and take a moment to be grateful for the time you have had to be mindful this morning and the benefits it will bring to your day.

Conclusion

Thank for making it through to the end of this book – *Mindfulness for Beginners: How Present Living Can Change Your Life*. I hope it was informative and was able to provide you with all of the tools you need to not just improve your mental state but your overall sense of well-being as well. Just because you have finished this book doesn't mean that you are now an expert on mindfulness, however. But by making mindfulness a part of every aspect of your life, you are able to reap a lot of the benefits it has to offer.

When you are first starting down the path to mindfulness, it is important to not expect too much too soon. A lifetime of instant gratification has likely destroyed your ability to focus long-term, so it is only natural that stray thoughts start bombarding you the second you try and clear your mind. Don't forget, this is a natural part of the process and as long as you persevere, there is no reason you shouldn't be able to take complete control of your thoughts in as little as a month's time.

Finally, while mindfulness mediation can be a great aid for a variety of mental illnesses, if you feel as though you are severely suffering from any of the conditions discussed in the proceeding chapters it is important to discuss treatment options with a professional rather than going it alone. While mindfulness can certainly help with many mental illnesses, it will always be more effective as part of a treatment plan created by a mental healthcare professional. For the majority of you, the fact that you are now aware of mindfulness is already a huge step in the right direction.

About the Author

Addison Fenn was born and raised in the city of Toronto, Ontario. While climbing the corporate ladder, Addison Fenn decided to move to the United States of America in search of better work opportunities. To maximize income so that more "clutter" can be purchased, Addison Fenn lived in one state for tax purposes while working in the neighboring state for higher wages.

Having come across the philosophy of minimalism, Addison Fenn dropped out of the consumerism rat-race to pursue the childhood dream of writing fantasy novels. Nowadays, Addison Fenn's life consists of freelance work, writing, and exploring the wonders of the great outdoors.

Made in the USA
Las Vegas, NV
04 August 2022

52718631R00115